JAVASCRIPT: OPTIMIZING NATIVE JAVASCRIPT

About the Author

Robert C. Etheredge is the founder of MiraVista Press and myWriterTools. He has been programming for over 30 years. He wrote his first programs on IBM punch cards, graduated to using paper tape programming U.S. Navy computers, and wrote his first commercial software on 5 1/4" Apple II floppy disks. He has designed or programmed more than 20 software products, and spent 16 years programming set top boxes and mobile devices using JavaScript and HTML. Recently he has been designing and programming JavaScript/HTML interfaces to process big data for health related applications.

JavaScript:
Optimizing Native JavaScript

Designing, programming, and debugging
native JavaScript applications

Using JavaScript, HTML, and CSS
in real projects with real deadlines and real constraints

Includes tips on UI design, optimization, and interviewing

BY
Robert C. Etheredge

MiraVista Press

JavaScript: Optimizing Native JavaScript
© Copyright 2017, 2020 by MiraVista Press

Published by MiraVista Press

MiraVista Press
P.O. Box 961
Orinda, CA 94563

Email: support@miravista.com
Web: http://www.miravista.com
http://www.nativeJavaScript.com

Printed in the United States of America.

DEDICATION

This book is dedicated to my children, and to my wife Cheri who has stood by me and put up with me for all these years.

"There are two ways of constructing a software design. One way is to make it so simple that there are obviously no deficiencies. And the other way is to make it so complicated that there are no obvious deficiencies."

- C.A.R. Hoare

Table of Contents

4
OBJECTS

5
HTML

6
CSS TECHNIQUES

11
LOADING PROGRAM FILES

12
TOOLS

13
DEBUGGING

A
INTERVIEWING

B
UI DESIGN

Introduction

Writing applications using JavaScript, HTML, and CSS can be fun and rewarding. JavaScript is a fairly easy language to learn and HTML/CSS makes it easy to create great looking interfaces without a lot of graphics experience. It is easy and inexpensive to get your own website up and running, or to make great apps for mobile devices. There is a large developer community online with many libraries and frameworks that you can download to help your development efforts.

However, this same low barrier to entry also makes it easy for bad JavaScript apps to be written. And by bad, I don't mean just inefficient code, but also apps that involve bad design and framework decisions. And this criticism is directed mainly at single-page, multi-screen JavaScript applications, and not just simple web pages. There are a number of reasons for these problems, including:

+ Novice programmers who have little or no training or experience in programming.

+ Designers and programmers coming from page-oriented web-site design.

+ Experienced C++ and Java programmers that don't really understand how best to write JavaScript applications.

+ Fast desktop computers with lots of memory that hide inefficiencies in code that may have to run on less powerful computers and mobile devices.

Why write about native JavaScript?

Many JavaScript websites and applications use any number of libraries and frameworks along with their native JavaScript code. In many cases, their use can shorten the development cycle and make the code easier to maintain by large development groups. However, I have found when writing high performance applications or highly customized applications that these libraries and frameworks often cause more trouble than they are worth. They add to the size of the code, slow things down, and often make maintenance harder because of having to track versions. Often, you will find a library to carry out a specific graphic or UI function only to find when you are almost done that it does not do exactly what you need and may be more trouble than it is worth to change it. Once modified, you no longer have a standard plug-in but rather customized code that you have to maintain. So this book concentrates on helping you write smaller and faster native JavaScript code.

There are lots of books about the many libraries and frameworks available for JavaScript development. If you develop websites and applications in JavaScript you most likely will use one or more of them in the course of your career. But remember that these libraries and frameworks are all themselves written in JavaScript and share all of the strengths and weaknesses pointed out in this book. Your knowledge of native JavaScript can only help you in your efforts.

Target audience of this book

Javascript: Optimizing Native JavaScript assumes that you have a good working knowledge of writing JavaScript applications or webpages using JavaScript, HTML, and CSS. You need to understand how those three systems interact and how to structure common applications. This book is not a language reference but more a collection of information to help you write more efficient JavaScript programs. Even if your application requires the use of frameworks and libraries, knowing how to code more efficient JavaScript will still be important. In these cases, you can still use frameworks and libraries for the majority of the code but native JavaScript where performance is important.

Based on real-life experience

I have been designing and programming JavaScript applications for more than 17 years. Most of this work was on applications designed for low memory and slow CPU platforms, such as set-top boxes and mobile devices. I found that many recommended solutions didn't necessarily make sense in real life situations. When you work on producing applications on deadlines, you tend to have different restrictions, methods, and goals.

Through years of examining JavaScript code, I discovered repeating conditions that led to the JavaScript/HTML code running poorly on the targeted platforms. These conditions included excessive number of objects, unnecessary date manipulation, excessive error checking, creation of excess garbage, using inefficient libraries, and poorly designed data structures. In many cases, I was able to reduce code size by up to 60% while easily doubling the speed of the code.

Write your code for others

Remember—someone else will very likely have to maintain or decipher your code. Or you may have to read someone else's code and hopefully be able to reuse it instead of starting over again. The clearer and simpler the code is written, the more likely it is to be reused—and this saves time and money.

Assume that whoever will be trying to make sense of your code does not know as much as you do. Be careful if you write code whose function is not obvious or could be ambiguous. If you are using some esoteric feature of JavaScript or some pattern that requires reading programming references to figure out how to use it—you probably shouldn't. There are always good reasons to use some of these advanced methods if your program requires it—just make sure you adequately document the code with clear in-line comments.

JavaScript, with its global namespace and interpreted functionality, is just different than most other languages. And writing code for companies that must meet real deadlines and have compact code that must perform on a variety of platforms is always a challenge.

Why is this book different from other books on JavaScript?

This is not a JavaScript reference book. It is not about using the latest frameworks and libraries. It does not cover esoteric coding solutions and algorithms, nor do I get into the inner workings of the JavaScript engine. This book assumes you already know JavaScript at some level and you can at least program simple pages. For more advanced JavaScript programmers, there are a number of good reference books available.

A lot of my experience is on set-top box devices that are limited in both CPU power and RAM, so writing small and fast JavaScript was imperative. But the same concepts apply even with faster PC browsers and mobile devices with more memory. Like everything else in computing, extra speed and memory is quickly consumed by larger pictures, video, and 3D graphics so you are almost right back where you started. Some applications or companies may require the use of specific frameworks or libraries, such as Angular or jQuery, but there are other times and projects where a more basic approach may be warranted.

My approach is practical. If you include code that is very difficult to understand (particularly if you don't comment it properly), then you probably shouldn't be including that code unless you can show that it gives you a clear advantage in speed or memory usage. This book should help you in real-life situations writing real code on a real schedule for real products.

Where is the code?

Some of the code referenced in this book can be found on our website at www.NativeJavascript. com. The comparison tests found throughout the book reference links at that website where the tests can be run. The speed tests are not definitive as absolute times vary greatly with browsers, browser versions, and computer systems. Plus you don't want to fixate on these times as many operations are so fast anyway that you can afford to take extra milliseconds and you may not want to sacrifice readability for speed. But if you know what types of operations and patterns are faster, then you can use them as your first choice, or use them when you choose to optimize.

Conventions in this book

The following conventions are used in this book.

- **Code**. Code examples are shown in a fixed pitch font, such as:

```
} else if (x==1) {
    elem.style.backgroundColor = cBackAlternate;
```

- **Performance examples.** Throughout the book, there are tables showing results from performance testing of various coding alternatives on different browsers. This shows the relative number of operations for each example and each browser. Higher numbers indicate better performance. These numbers only make sense in relation to each other as they are the times to perform thousands of each operation and in many cases the numbers have been shortened for readability. Beneath each table is listed the URL where you can run the performance test yourself. The numbers make more sense when comparing operations on the same browsers rather than trying to compare times across browsers.

⏱	PERFORMANCE TESTING	OPS (bigger is better)		
		Safari	Chrome	Firefox
1. test 1		711	1,350	1,312
2. test 2		702	3,330	1,634

Test 3-5: http://www.nativeJavascript.com/tests/Test-Sample
NOTE: Performance numbers listed for all the tests in this book may change with each new browser version release. Some operations may get faster, while others may even get slower. Test them again before relying on them in your app.

- **Browsers Tested:** The various performance and memory tests shown in the book were generally done with the following browsers, though exact version numbers were constantly changing. Running the same tests again may produce different results due to newer versions of browsers, different computer speeds, other applications running at the same time, etc. However, unless a specific browser has optimized a certain feature (or degraded it), the relative results should be similar. We tested on both Windows and Macintosh computers. The versions used for our tests are listed below. You can run the tests from our website on whatever browser you want.

  - Chrome: 55.0
  - Safari: 9.1
  - FireFox: 50.1.0

Terms and abbreviations in this book

- **API**: Application Program Interface. Describes the exact specification allowing applications to communicate with other applications and servers.

- **app**: An abbreviation for *application*.

- **camelCase**: Describes a common way to represent variable names by uppercase letters inside the word to make it easier to read.

- **DOM**: Document Object Model. Describes the elements making up your displayed HTML.

- **GC**: Garbage collection. An automatic process carried out by browsers to free up memory used by objects that are no longer in use.

- **IDE**: Integrated Development Environment. A software application designed to assist programmers in writing and running code, such as Eclipse or IntelliJ IDEA.

- **JSON**: JavaScript Object Notation. A common data representation format used to transfer data to and from JavaScript applications.

- **JSONP**: JSON with Padding. A method to send and receive JSON objects between different browser locations (cross-domain). It requires that JSON object to be wrapped in a function statement.

- **UI**: User interface. This describes the visual representation of the application and how it interfaces with the user.

1
Basic Principles

There are a number of principles you should keep in mind during all stages of your application process, from design to implementation. These principles help drive your coding style and influence all the decisions you have to make during the project. I have been surprised at the number of times they are ignored.

Problems often arise when you are interfacing between different groups involved in the application process. If these groups are not aware of the limitations (and strengths) of JavaScript/HTML, it is often easy for them to overlook some basic design principles. The main outside groups that you will be concerned with are:

- **Designers**. If designers treat each application UI screen as a separate HTML screen, then you will have problems designing an optimized application. They must understand that you are usually better off sharing as many screens and code as possible. Even if your application loads a number of separate screens, you are still better off using shared files since they can be cached for faster loading.

- **Server programmers**. They may often ignore what is best for the application in designing their API's and data structures. They need to understand that their data packets have to be small and appropriate to the needs of the application. You need to work together to maximize the amount of data that can be cached by avoiding unique URL strings. The server data should be formatted to avoid having the client application reformat and remap any data. One of the advantages of the JSON data format is that it can be converted directly into JavaScript objects, reducing code size and garbage production. Parsing XML in JavaScript is much more difficult.

Principles

All things being equal—smaller and faster is better, unless it makes the code hard to understand or maintain. You often don't know what other programs or libraries will be loaded at the same time as your code, so make it as small and fast as you can. Even an extra 20 or 30 milliseconds of execution time may cause your UI to suffer in some cases, especially in fast-scrolling situations.

Size still matters

Smaller is better and bigger is...well, bigger. It is easy to fall into complacency when programming your application on a powerful desktop computer with lots of memory. But you should always strive to reduce the memory footprint of every function that you code. This applies to the objects and arrays that you create, images that you place in your UI's, and all the data structures that you have to download or create. The reasons you need to keep it small include:

- Mobile device users have to download code and data using limited bandwidth that they often have to pay for. And downloads over the cellular network are going to be slower than what you get on your regular Ethernet connection. Your users want their mobile applications to load and become functional as quickly as possible.

- You don't necessarily know what other app or data will be loaded at the same time your app is. This is true of frameworks and libraries that may be loaded by your app, or by other apps that are running on the device at the same time.

- Creating and destroying strings, or loading and deleting data, creates memory garbage. The way JavaScript is designed, you are unable to force a garbage collection (GC) from the code but must rely on the browser to decide when to force a GC. If this happens at the wrong time, such as when the user is fast scrolling a table, the UI can be adversely affected. So the rule is—just don't make the garbage to begin with.

Speed still matters

Faster is better. You should try to write all your functions to be as fast as possible while keeping the code readable. This does not mean optimizing your code at every step of the project. There is a good argument for waiting until your code logic is in place before optimizing your code. You often won't know what optimizing strategies are best until you have all pieces of the logic in place. But that doesn't mean that you can't apply the best principles as you are writing your code. The methods discussed in later chapters, such as using local variables or declaring an array length variable outside of the `for` loop, should always be used.

Flatter is better

Make your UI designs as flat as possible. This is much more important for single screen applications. Design your screens to include common navigation and filtering controls on the same screen without creating series of nested menus that the user must navigate to carry out required functions.

The server shouldn't make UI decisions

Make sure that the data delivered by the server doesn't restrict or change the functionality of your UI. If the server gives you dates in the wrong format, or unused data, or fields that are unnecessarily long, they are impacting the performance of your application. If the server can't give you enough data at one time to let you fill in your scrollable screens, your user's experience may suffer. If the server gives you excessive data that must be garbage collected on your end, your performance will suffer. Make sure the server team is involved in your design procedure early so they can deliver optimized and appropriate information. I had projects where the server team refused to optimize the data format delivered to the client, resulting in 160mb of data having to be delivered to a mobile device, greatly affecting the user experience. I was able to optimize that to a 3mb payload that the client received almost immediately, allowing almost immediate scrolling of all the data. Think of all the effort you may spend to minify your JavaScript content, but then you go and load huge data files that are unnecessarily large. Other incorrect server choices involve having dates formatted on the server instead of letting the user interface format them according to the user's preferences, and sub-optimal uses of booleans, strings, and numbers.

Share, share, share...

Share code and screens as much as possible. I am not talking about writing your code to be reusable in other projects. That is a separate subject open for debate as it tends to make your project take longer. What I am talking about is making sure that you don't copy and paste the same routine in multiple places in your code. If you have to do the same thing more than once, spend the time to make one good function that can be called from several places. Put some more time in designing your application up front and create single functions that can be used in several places. The same also applies to your HTML code which can have more impact on your application's performance. Be careful when laying out your HTML screens so you reuse them as often as possible and avoid continual altering or destroying the DOM tree.

Make the appropriate trade-offs

There are almost always trade-offs when you are writing code. Your job as a programmer is to optimize for the proper value when you have a choice. The trade-offs are usually between:

- memory use
- execution speed
- code readability

There hopefully will be many cases in which you can optimize for all three values. In other cases, you will have to analyze whether your UI demands fast execution, or whether you need to conserve memory. If you select a method that results in code that is more difficult to read, make sure that you properly comment the section as much as needed. Keep in mind a few general rules when optimizing your code:

- Do not optimize prematurely. However, that doesn't mean that you shouldn't try to use best practices all the time.
- Code readability is always important so be sure to comment any section of code that may be difficult to understand. Comments can be easily removed by minifiers when your app is released.
- Focus on 'low hanging fruit' first. This follows Pareto's 80-20 principle. You can usually get 80% of the benefit from concentrating on just 20% of the code. Profile your code to determine where memory is used and where performance suffers. Then focus on those areas. Obvious areas of concern are recursive functions and loops.

How many lines of code do you write?

If you are ever asked how many lines of code you wrote, replying with a large number is not necessarily a good thing. Be proud of writing a smaller number of lines—just make them very good lines of code. As Mark Twain (or Blaise Pascal) is said to have commented—"I am sorry this letter is so long but I didn't have the time to make it shorter."

2

JavaScript Formatting

First, we'll go over the simple, but often contentious, subject of formatting your JavaScript code. This seems like a simple topic, but proper formatting greatly affects how easily others can read and maintain your code. It is particularly important when you have more than one programmer working on the same code base and how your version control software works. I include a number of suggestions here based on my experience with writing and particularly with sharing JavaScript code. Because of JavaScript's unique interpretive nature and global context structure, many of these items are more important than they are in compiled languages. It is important to decide on guidelines that will be used across your products. Your programming environment and code validator that you use will also influence your style as you want to be able to leverage those two tools.

NOTE: Some IDE environments or code validators may automatically format or at least suggest formatting changes to your code. These tools may decide a number of formatting conventions for you. You may want to decide on a formatting tool first and base your formatting guidelines on that tool.

Strict mode

JavaScript 1.8.5 added a new feature called *strict mode*. To invoke it, you include the expression "use strict" in your code at the beginning of the script or function where you want it to apply, using the following line of code:

```
"use strict";
```

It is designed to make it harder to write "bad" JavaScript code. Some of the sections in this book assume you are not running in strict mode. When set, strict mode will throw errors in the following situations:

- Using a variable before it is declared
- Deleting a variable or object using the `delete` method
- Using the `with` statement
- Restrictions on use of other variable names
- `arguments.callee` is no longer supported

Comments

Comment style

Even something as simple as commenting needs to be handled consistently. In JavaScript, you can use two main types of comments and you may read books or articles recommending each type. Note: You need to use a different type of comment for CSS and HTML files. The comment types for your JavaScript code are:

1. // Two slashes anywhere on a line treats the remainder of that line as a comment. You can use this for blocks of code (each line starting with //), single line comments, or comments on the end of a line after the code.

2. /* */ Any code placed between the starting /* tag and an ending */ tag is treated as a comment. These tags can surround multiple lines of code, or just one line.

I strongly recommend using the first type of comments (//) in your code for three main reasons:

1. If you have a /* */ block and insert another /* */ block inside of it, it will most likely throw a JavaScript error.

2. When you do global searches for variable names, it makes it much easier to find the important strings that are real code and not commented code if you always use //. Otherwise, any code that is inside a block comment may look like valid code.

3. /* */ may fail if it surrounds regular expressions like: `var rgex = /c*/;`

One good reason for using block comments may be for temporary commenting out a block of code for testing purposes, knowing that you are going to remove the comments later.

What comments to include?

The amount of commenting should be dictated by your programming style, the clarity of your code, and the requirements of your project. Since you most likely will be compressing your code before it is deployed, you don't normally have to worry about the space taken up by your comments. However, excess or extraneous comments can actually make your code harder to read. Make sure you comment any places where the logic is not clear to anyone new to the code (or even to you 6 months later.). You can place comments above logic branch points for clarity, and additional comments to the right of lines that need explanation, such as:

```
//USER HASN'T ENTERED VALUE
if (x==0) then {
   elem.style.backgroundColor = cBackMain;

//USER HAS PICKED SECONDARY COLOR
} else if (x==1) {
   elem.style.backgroundColor = cBackAlternate;
}
var rx=regex(/^\d{5}/);    //match 5 digits at start of line
```

But please don't add comments that don't add anything if the code is self-explanatory, such as:

```
lastIndex = 5;              //set last index to 5        UNNECESSARY!
```

Comments indicating ToDo items

Something else I have found very useful when coding a large project, particularly if there are other programmers involved, is to use your comments to communicate to the other programmers or to make notes to yourself. I include comments with my initials anywhere I have a question or know that I need to go back and fix something. I have also included the initials of another programmer in a section where I know they need to do something. Just keep your tag (i.e. your initials) consistent so you can easily do a global search to find all the comments. Be sure to comment any temporary or debugging code so you can make sure it is removed before final. Some IDE environments automatically support and track TODO type comments for similar usage. I might have comments like:

```
//RCE: this function needs to be optimized
//RCE: I am not sure what the possible values are here
//DD: Can you add the appropriate code in here?
//RCE: temporary test - take out before final
```

Comments for documentation such as JSDoc

Documenting your code always seems to be a real pain and something you put off until the very end, or sometimes after the end, of the project. Depending on your project, this can be a real detriment. If items are not documented right away, you may have trouble remembering exactly how functions work or why they were written. If you are writing modules that will be used by other programmers, or have a published API, then proper documentation is crucial.

There are a number of products that simplify your JavaScript code documentation task, such as JSDoc or YUIDoc. These rely on the programmer embedding comments using a format specific to the tool, such as:

```
/**
 * Method description about the following method. Can be several lines.
 *
 * @method nameOfMethod
 * @param {String} objname Description of this string.
 * @param {Object} obj Description of object that is passed in
 * @return {Boolean} Returns true on success
 */
```

Whether you want to use one of these methods is up to you and your project team. Most likely the person responsible for producing the formal documentation for the project will have the final say. The advantages of using one of these methods include:

- They allow the programmer to communicate complicated information to the documentation team.
- They force the programmer to properly document their methods, often resulting in better and more concise API's.
- Some IDE's take advantage of embedded documentation to give you popup help, variable typing information, or code completion.
- If done concurrently with your code, then you will have your documentation ready when your code is done.

However, there are some disadvantages to this approach. Your team (or yourself if working alone) will have to decide on the correct approach. Some disadvantages include:

- It takes discipline on each programmer's part to properly fill out each comment section.

- You have to be careful that comment sections aren't just copied and pasted without the proper changes being made.

- They can make the actual code a lot harder to read. Large sections of comments can make it harder to make sense of your code. Some IDE's make it easy to hide comment sections.

- If several programmers are working on the same project, they may have different documentation styles that the documentation team will have to reconcile before producing the final formal documentation.

- Programmers tend to give comments a lower priority than the actual code. The project lead or documentation team will have to spend time to ensure that the comments are properly added and updated.

- If the embedded comments are relied upon to produce final documentation without an additional and detailed editing pass by the programmer, they can easily produce incorrect documentation which can be worse than no documentation.

- The documentation team most likely has to add more details to their documentation than is found in the embedded comments, such as more details, examples, corner cases. This means they must understand the code or have it carefully explained.

Your team will have to decide on a consistent solution and ensure that it is followed. At minimum, you should have a way to identify which functions and variables need to be documented and which ones are essentially private. When in doubt, add comments as you write your code. You can always take them out or redo them later.

Punctuation

Semi-colons

Unfortunately, the JavaScript spec did not require semi-colons to be used to terminate every line, but you should ensure that you use them that way. Even though you can get away with not using them, you most likely will be tripped up when using a closure compiler or minifier on your code. These can create error conditions if semi-colons aren't used to terminate your lines properly. The following code may be misinterpreted if you run it through a compiler since the compiler will add a semi-colon after the word `return` which is not what you want. It will return nothing instead of your object with the index value. This is another reason not to place your braces on separate lines, discussed in a following section. Some IDE environments will also flag code that is missing terminating semi-colons.

```
function doThis(str) {                               Bad Code!
    return
    {
        index: 1
    };
}
```

Operator precedence in formulas

JavaScript, like all computer languages, has a set order it uses to analyze formulas containing operators. For example, multiplication operations are carried out before addition operations. You can find the list in any number of articles or books. You should err on the side of being overly precise, even if it means a few extra characters. Don't assume that everyone reading your code remembers the order of precedence for operators like + * / ^ etc. Just make it clearer by putting in parenthesis wherever they are needed. Do you immediately know how the following formula is calculated?

```
var prec = x + y / 4 - 2 * z % 5;
```

Even if you do, putting in parenthesis where appropriate can only help a reader understand what you are trying to do. It also wouldn't hurt to add some comments clarifying what the formula is attempting to do.

Location of braces

This is seemingly trivial formatting decision that creates heated arguments every time it is discussed. Do I write my code like:

```
if (a == b)
{
    var a = 5:
}
```

Or like:

```
if (a == b) {
    var a = 5;
}
```

To me, the case is closed. The second method is much more compact, easier to read, and friendlier to some code analysis tools like JSLint. There is an advantage to being able to see more code on the screen at one time as you page through your program. The same rule applies to other blocks such as *for* loops and *switch* statements. Unfortunately, it will probably still be a subject of debate every place you work. Programmers coming from different languages tend to prefer the first style.

Strings—Single or double quotes

In JavaScript, you can normally use single or double quotes interchangeably. There are two cases where you have to pay attention to which you are using:

1. There are times you have to have quotes inside quotes, such as setting HTML from JavaScript, like:

   ```
   var str = '<div style="left:10px;">text</div>';
   ```

   There you will have to use one type for the outside quotes and the other type for the inside one. You can do it either way for this example, but it is usually better to use single quotes for the outside string quotes when making HTML strings.

2. JSON. The JSON standard specifies that all key-value pairs should be in double, not single, quotes.

In general, you should be as consistent as you can across your entire code base. Don't arbitrarily alternate between styles. One problem that arises if you are inconsistent, or if programmers working on the same code base use different methods, involves global searching. Often you are looking for a specific word in a string that may appear in several places, so you may try to search for (*"string*). If you are unsure of what quote symbols were used, you will also have to search for (*'string*). And you may also close strings you are entering with the incorrect symbol if you are not consistent, although many IDE environments catch this error.

Lines and spacing

Line length

You should try to keep the length of your code lines to 80 characters or less. It is often advantageous to be able to see your entire line of code without horizontal scrolling. You can break a long line if necessary, usually by adding a break after an operator like a comma. The next line should continue with an indention level that matches its logical location.

Tabs or spaces?

This argument is on the same lines as "paper or plastic?" This is entirely up to your company's or team's policy. It usually depends on what the other programmers prefer and what your source control software does with tabs in source code. If tabs are used, they are usually set to either two or four spaces. Most text editors or SDK's have options covering how they handle tabs and spaces. They can be set up to expand tabs to spaces when saving or opening, if desired. The most important setting will be in your source control system. You want to make sure that file comparison tools treat tabs and spaces as being equal, or simply ignore whitespace.

Whitespace around operators and variables

The issue about whether to include spaces around variables and operators is nullified somewhat by the use of closure compilers or minifiers that remove extra whitespace. So there is really no good reason not to include some extra space around these items in order to make your code more readable. So, instead of:

```
var x=2;                                    Not Recommended!
if(x==2) {
```

use:

```
var x = 2;
if (x == 2) {
```

Some tools like JSLint prefer the second method and will display warning messages for the first method. However, adding spaces around parameters in function declarations can be harder to read, though some formatters prefer that format. Instead of:

```
function funcName ( a, b ){
```

I prefer spacing to look like:

```
function funcName(a, b) {
```

Indenting your code

Make sure you indent all of your code consistently based on logical levels. Many editors and SDK's do this automatically. Just make sure that it gets done. You may want to indent each level by either two or four spaces. You also want all braces that are logically connected to have the same indent level. It will make it much easier to check your code for unmatched braces or bad logic. This also applies to your HTML code. So your code should look something like:

```
for (var i = 0; i < 10; i++) {
  for (var j = 0; j < 5; j++) {
    if (i == 0) {
      //more code here
    }
  }
}
```

Lining up equal signs

Another formatting option you may see often in third party code, and one that I tend to use, is to line up the equal signs or object properties when successive lines are very similar. If you are compressing your code, these spaces will be removed and sometimes the extra indent makes it easier to read the code. It might look like:

```
var thisnum  = 5;
var idx      = 12;
var str      = 'name';
var obj      = {
  prop1:    'value',
  dateprop: 123,
  idx:      1
};
```

Variable and function names

There are a number of naming conventions that are generally accepted as well as some others than are sometimes contentious. There are a few restrictions about naming that are enforced by JavaScript engines, including:

- **Case-sensitive.** JavaScript names are case-sensitive. Thus, *thisVar* and *ThisVar* are treated as separate variable names.

- **Reserved words.** There are a number of words that are reserved by the JavaScript language. You can see a complete list at https://developer.mozilla.org/en-US/docs/Web/JavaScript/Reference/Reserved_Words

- **Special characters.** Names should consist of letters (A-Z, a-z), numbers (0-9), and the underscore (_). Don't use other special characters and I would avoid international and Unicode symbols as they may be misinterpreted and are harder to search. I would also avoid using the dollar sign ($), even though it is valid, as it is used by frameworks as an alias and could be misinterpreted. Numbers are valid but may not start a variable or function name.

All other naming suggestions rely on coding convention and handling the global namespace of JavaScript. As is true of other formatting suggestions, the programming team should decide on a standard and enforce that standard.

Global namespace

JavaScript code runs in a global namespace. This means that all your separate functions, variables, objects, methods, and modules share a common root, the *window* object. Nothing prevents you from adding your names to the global namespace. If you declare variables outside of your functions, or inside a function but without a *var* statement, they will be placed in this global namespace. There are a number of good reasons to avoid placing your variable and function names in the global namespace, including:

- They can be easily overwritten or deleted by another program or process that is loaded by your application, including libraries and frameworks. Or you may even have two of your own functions relying on the same global variable without realizing that another function is changing it.

- Relying on global variables and functions can make your code harder to maintain. They can discourage encapsulation and code organization that will make your modules and functions easier to debug or reuse.

- Accessing a global variable directly from within a function is slower than using a local variable, or a local copy of the global variable.

- If your project is using global variables, you have to make sure you have a strict naming convention in place that prevents programmers from declaring variables with the same name. You should be able to assign a company related prefix to each item in the global space, such as `mvModel` and `mvViews`.

Global namespace solutions

There are a number of solutions to preventing problems when using the global namespace. Normally, you have to place at least one object in the global space, if just to hold all of your variables and functions. But remember this is not a magic solution—now you have one name that can still be overwritten, resulting in your entire application being deleted. So you still have to be careful no matter what you do. Your solution depends on the type of application you are writing. If you are writing a specific app where you control all of the content that will be added to the global namespace, you may pick a different solution that an application that has to handle different 3rd party libraries or code being added to that space. The solutions to consider include:

- Using objects to hold your variables and functions. You can use one global object (which can contain multiple objects itself), or a small set of global objects to keep most of your names out of the global namespace. Thus, you might have code that looks like:

```
var globalObj = {
    fname:    "name",
    city:     "city",
    showName: function() {
        console.log("Name: " + this.fname);
    }
};
```

This places just one name, `globalObj`, in the global namespace. The same approach would work if you create a Constructor function that creates new instances of objects.

* Using closures to keep your variables and functions out of the global namespace. This is a common method that both protects the global namespace and allows you to keep certain variables or functions essentially "private." There are several ways to write these functions, from having a public object with accessible methods, to having a completely anonymous function that is run once when you start up and never used again. They may look like:

```
var nafDate = (function(){
    var localvar    = 5;
    var fname       = "name";
    var localMethod = function() {
       console.log("Name: " + fname);
    };
    var globalMethod = function() {
      localMethod();
    };
    return {
        fname:          fname,
        globalMethod:   globalMethod
    };
}) ();
```

This creates a global object called `nafDate` that has only two items that can be accessed outside the function, `fname` and `globalMethod`, which were both returned when the object was created. The last line of the declaration that contains `}) ();` results in this function being immediately executed when it is read in, creating the `nafDate` object. The `localMethod` function cannot be accessed outside of the `nafDate` object.

* No matter what approach you take, you have to worry about your global names being overwritten by other code. So, pay attention to the naming of your global objects. I have used a method of assigning a unique lower case prefix to each functional part of your program that might have names in the global space.

Lowercase and uppercase characters in names

There are some commonly accepted conventions for naming your JavaScript variables and functions. Unless you have some strong reasons to adopt another method, I would recommend using these conventions as it will make your code easier to read by other programmers.

* **Constructors**. Constructor functions should start with a capital letter. This makes it easy to determine what the function is used for. They should look like:

```
function MakeView()
```

* **Regular names**. Regular variables and function names should start with lowercase letters and should be camelcased if needed for clarity, such as:

```
function displayScreen()
var dateObj = {};
```

* **Constants**. JavaScript used to have no data type for *constants*. You could simulate constants and declare variable names with all uppercase letters to make them stand out. However, most browsers now support the `const` statement to be used in place of `var`. Variables declared with `const` cannot be redeclared or have their value changed. So you could declare your constant values like:

```
var kENTER   = 13;   //this can be changed
const kLEFT  = 37;   //this cannot be changed
```

- **Use of underscore.** A common convention for methods and properties inside objects that are not "public" or available outside the function is to start the name with an underscore, and then follow the naming rules above. Thus, your constructor for `MakeView` may have a local variable named: `var _netWorth` that is referenced inside that object or closure only. There is nothing magic about the underscore—JavaScript doesn't interpret these names any differently. However, if you don't have complete closure around the variable where it could be referenced outside the function if someone knows the name, such as `view._netWorth`, then it makes it easier to find variables used improperly. If you are careful to keep your names out of the global space, this technique is less useful. You may see it in the code from other programmers so you should understand its usual purpose.
- **Characters to avoid.** I avoid using the letter "l" (L) or "o" (O) in my names unless they are part of a recognizable word, such as `fullName` or `logo`. I particularly avoid using these for single letter variables, or at ends of names where they may be mistaken for the number zero (0) or one (1).

```
var logor = "logoright.gif";
var logol = "logoleft.gif";                          Avoid!
```

Length of names

Get used to using short names. It saves space but more importantly, it keeps you always thinking about keeping your code small. Remember that since you will most likely be compressing your code before putting the code into production, you can freely add comments to your code instead of using very long names. By keeping your names short to begin with, you reduce the need to have your minifier refactor all variable names. But don't make them so short or common that they become hard to find during global searches. Shorter names also are easier to type and reduce the chances of typing errors.

Variable names in loops

The convention in JavaScript code seems to be to use 'i' as a variable name in loops and not 'x'. Some coders like to use more descriptive names, like ctr or titleIdx but that is normally not needed unless you have an extremely long loop. Use `i` (and `j,k,m` if you need more variables inside the loop) but avoid use lowercase `L` (`l`) or the letter `'o'`. I think you will find it easier to read your code if you are consistent in this naming. Is this some hard and fast rule? No...just keep it in mind.

Names to avoid

There are some names you should avoid using for your variables and functions to avoid possible problems. These include:

- Local variable names inside a function that are the same names as global variables, even if the capitalization is different. This is just asking for trouble.
- Names that are the same as any HTML element ID names. This produces unpredictable results, particularly across browsers. Even if you think it may help you, don't rely on it.

Some browsers will allow you to just reference the element ID directly instead of using `document.getElementById`. The following example assumes you have an HTML element with an id like: `<div id="eSPLASH">`. This code:

```
console.log("getelem: " + document.getElementById("eSPLASH"));
console.log("varname: " + eSPLASH);
eSPLASH = 12;
console.log("getelem: " + document.getElementById("eSPLASH"));
console.log("varname: " + eSPLASH);
```

produces this output:

```
getelem: [object HTMLDivElement]
varname: [object HTMLDivElement]
getelem: [object HTMLDivElement]
varname: 12
```

* Short names that are part of reserved words, common function names, or JavaScript function names. If you insist on naming some variable `ById`, then your searches will find all instances of that name, including the multiple instances of document.getElementById you have in your code. The same goes for any other short common name. This gets really bad if you use short names like "loc" or "nam" or similar names. It will take a long time to sift through your extended code base to find the correct ones.

The *var* declaration statement

The use and positioning of the `var` statement is another subject of heated debate. There are several methods often pushed as the correct way to do this. The use of `var` is very important, as it keeps variables and function names from being added to the global namespace when not desired and accessing local variables is faster. `var` statements are *hoisted* in the functions they appear in. This means that no matter where the `var` statement occurs, it is essentially treated as if it was at the top of the function. However, only the declaration is hoisted—not the value assignment. It you try to access the variable before you assign a value, it will be `undefined`. Consider the following code that is not contained in a function:

```
var globalidx = 9;          //this is a global variable
var idx      = 5;           //this is a global variable
function test() {
    console.log(idx);        //this prints 'undefined'
    console.log(globalidx);  //this will print 9
    var idx = 2;             //this will be local variable
    console.log(idx);        //this will print 2
}
test();
console.log(idx);            //this prints 5 - the global value
```

When the `test` function is run, the first printing of `idx` is undefined because although the declaration of `idx` inside the function was hoisted, overriding the global value, the value assignment of 2 was not. The second printing displays the value of 2 which was assigned the line before. When the last statement prints, it displays the global value of `idx`. So, what are your options for positioning your `var` statements? It is generally accepted that you should declare all your vars at the top of each function to minimize errors. So the following options all assume that you place all vars at the start.

- **Method 1.** Declare all variables using one `var` statement on one line, with or without assignments.

  ```
  var a,b,c;
  ```

  or

  ```
  var a = 1, b = 2, c = 3;
  ```

- **Method 2.** Use one `var` statement but put each declaration on a separate line.

  ```
  var a = 1,
      b = 2,
      c = 3;
  ```

- **Method 3.** Use a separate `var` statement for each declaration and put on a separate line.

  ```
  var a = 1;
  var b = 2;
  var c = 3;
  ```

Based on my experience, I recommend the last method. You can additionally list them in alphabetical order to make them easier to find if you want to spend a little extra work. The reasons I recommend this method include:

- The declarations are easier to read. Long statements with multiple declarations make it hard to find the new variables, especially if you have complicated assignments.

- You reduce the chance of errors in future changes. If, for example, someone changes the first comma in method 2 after the `a` assignment to a semi-colon, the rest of the variables will be assigned to the global namespace, possible without you being aware of the change.

- If you use method 2, then when you do global searches for variable names, it will not be clear what that line of code means since you won't see the var statement.

Use of *vars* in for loops

I think there are a few other potentially confusing uses of `var` declarations. Again, these are not requirements of any nature; just suggestions.

- **Loops.** I think it is safer to put the var declaration statement directly in the for loop statement. That way, any global search that finds that line will verify that the variable is indeed declared locally which is mandatory for good code optimization. So your statement should look like:

  ```
  for (var i = 0; i < 12; i++) {
  ```

- **Multiple declarations in loops.** I also think the following style is potentially confusing and hard to read. Just go ahead and put the second declaration on its own line. Instead of:

  ```
  for (var i = 0; x = 4; i < 12; i++) {
  ```

  use

  ```
  var x = 4;
  for (var i = 0; i < 12; i++) {
  ```

Bad formatting choices

There are several format variations that are legal JavaScript but which I think are examples of bad coding. They can easily be misinterpreted or incorrectly changed by another programmer that misreads the code.

One bad example that is legal but may result in errors is:

```
for (var i = 0; i < 10; i++)                    Don't Do This!
    console.log("i" + i);
```

Another common coding convention often seen in books and articles looks like the following but is also a prime source of errors:

```
if (a == b)                                     Don't Do This!
    //Do this
else if (c == d)
    //Do that
```

These are really bad coding examples (yes, I know, they are perfectly legal.) Just get used to using braces all the time. They take up almost no room and keep everything very clear. If a second line of code has to be added in one of the sections, it won't create an error. So the last example should look like:

```
if (a == b) {
    //Do this
} else if (c == d) (
    //Do that
}
```

Personally, I think one-line statements are ok if they are self-contained. They may make it easier to read the entire function. However, you may want to have even these simple statements be written with braces to allow for additional statements to be easily added later. An example of a one-line statement is:

```
if (a == b) x = y;
```

Code compilers and minifiers

There are a number of tools you can use to compress your JavaScript code before deployment. The list includes Google's Closure Compiler, JSMIN, UglifyJS, and YUI Compressor. Most of them have different options to control how much optimization is desired during the compile. They work by doing one or more of the following operations on your code:

- Remove all comments
- Remove all extra spaces and tabs
- Combine all your lines of code into one line
- Obfuscate variable and function names to very short 1 or 2 character names.
- Pre-process logic where possible, such as changing:
  ```
  var d = 5;
  callFunction(5 + 3 + d);
  ```
  to
  ```
  callFunction(13);
  ```

The main goal is to produce a smaller file that will be downloaded and parsed faster while taking up less bandwidth. I have been using one form or another of this type of tool for more than ten years. I have always been comfortable using the tool to remove comments and spaces, but am usually reluctant to have it perform the more advanced obfuscation and minification. You will get most of the compression by removing spaces and comments and I feel that using the advanced features are often not worth the risk. The advanced minification makes more sense for well-tested and often-used third party libraries, or functions of yours that don't change and have been properly tested.

The items to consider when deciding what level of compression to use include:

- Your testing cycle. You will normally be writing and testing the full, uncompressed code but running the compressor only when you do official releases. This means that the released code is potentially a completely different code base with possibly different code paths. You need to take this into account when you set up your testing schedule. Sometimes just loading certain files faster when they are smaller may uncover timing errors.

- Debugging. If you or your users are debugging the minified code, you will be using the minified code. This is almost impossible to properly debug as you can't really understand the code and all errors will be reported as being on the same line. The good news here is that most debug consoles have a way to "pretty-print" the code. In the Chrome debugger, you can go to the Sources tab, open the source file and click the { } icon in the lower left corner. This will reformat the code onto separate lines so you can read it.

- Since most of your JavaScript code will be accessible to anyone running your application, it is difficult to protect your intellectual property. Having your code minified greatly helps obfuscate your code to make it harder for others to reuse your creative output.

- Last, but not least, advanced optimization runs the risk of introducing errors into your code, mainly because of the non-typed nature of JavaScript. Function names might be located in strings, or made from concatenating strings. If the compiler attempts to replace variable names with shorter alternatives, you may create errors. Consider the following code:

```
bigPic = {
    drawLine: function(idx) {
        console.log("in drawLine " + idx);
    }
};
bigPic.drawLine(1);
bigPic["drawLine"](2);
bigPic['drawLine'](3);
var a = "drawLine";
bigPic[a](4);
bigPic["draw" + "Line"](5);
```

when run, this produces the following output:

```
in drawLine 1
in drawLine 2
in drawLine 3
in drawLine 4
in drawLine 5
```

When run through the YUI Compiler, you will get similar results. However, running it through Google's Closure Compiler in Advanced mode produces the following code:

```
BigPic={a:function(a){console.log("in drawLine "+a)}}; BigPic.a(1);
BigPic.drawLine(2);BigPic.drawLine(3);BigPic.drawLine(4);
BigPic.drawLine(5);
```

This creates JavaScript errors as soon as you run it. So if you decide to use the more advanced compiler options, you need to carefully inspect your code to make sure you don't create these kinds of errors.

"Measuring programming progress by lines of code is like measuring aircraft building progress by weight."

- Bill Gates

3

JavaScript

This chapter covers JavaScript commands and operators. It is not a reference manual nor does it cover all commands and operators. There are other books and websites that offer this information. It does, however, cover the real-life usage of JavaScript in creating applications for JavaScript enabled devices and computers. I discuss ways to optimize your code so that it is smaller and faster. I do not rely upon third party frameworks to handle needed functionality—everything is written in native JavaScript. If you can understand and write that, then you can understand and write using any of the frameworks. JavaScript libraries and frameworks are just more layers of code—they have to be bigger and slower, but they do help standardize functionality particularly when used on projects supported by many programmers. They have advantages, particularly if you are a novice programmer, since they are widely used and should be error-free. But they are not magic and they tend to have many cross-dependencies.

JavaScript versions

JavaScript was developed in 1995 and is known by its un-trademarked name as ECMAScript. It has evolved over the years through many major version releases and is currently available in flavors of version 1.7 or 1.8. Each browser (IE, Firefox, Chrome, Opera, etc.) have their own implementation and don't all support the same features so you have to be careful in what JavaScript features you rely on if you need cross-browser compatibility. To be safe, you need to either support the oldest version used by the browsers you must support, or special case your code based on the browser version. Many of the frameworks and libraries that are available today have cross-browser support. Older versions of Internet Explorer, in particular, have many known incompatibilities with other browsers. Google has an open source JavaScript engine called V8 which is used in their Chrome browser.

The latest ECMA Script version 6 is supported on most browsers but with varying degrees of compliance. You can find a number of sites on the Internet that list compatibilities by feature and by browser. You should be very careful relying on these new features in your application. Some items might be useful like the new `let` and `const` declarations. You can use websites like `http://www.caniuse.com` to verify which features work on which browsers.

Performance

We have discussed performance in most chapters of this book and, in many cases, listed results from actual tests run on several browsers. In many cases, running tests thousands of times with various options to find one that runs milliseconds faster is not going to magically make your application perform better. But you should keep the general concepts in mind so that you code as efficiently as possibly. This chapter discusses a few more issues about performance that you should keep in mind as you design and program your application. And keep in mind that the tests recorded throughout this book are done on specific browser versions available at the time. Browsers are continually changing and the test results can change in either direction, either becoming slower or faster. Be sure to use tools like Google PageSpeed to improve your code.

Variable types

JavaScript is not a typed language. This does cause some problems and also means your IDE, if you use one, can't be as optimized in the same way it would be for a regular typed languages. There are solutions out there now like TypeScript, and future plans for Javascript itself to address this shortcoming. But in the meantime, you can use this "feature" to your advantage if you are careful. You just need to always be aware of how the JavaScript operators work and what the values are that you are testing. Even though variables are not strictly typed, there are several general types of variables that can be created, including:

- strings
- numbers
- objects
- booleans

You need to aware of types of variables when you try to perform operations on them or you may get unpredictable results. Javascript does try to coerce variables of one type to another where possible, such as adding a number to the end of a string, but you have to understand what is happening or you may get the wrong results. If you stay aware of what format your data and input fields are in, then you should be able to properly handle it in your code.

Caution with global variable declarations

First of all, you should keep global declarations to a minimum. You can declare some higher level object names as globals but try to avoid using global declaration for variable names. Assuming that you must declare some global variables, note that there are three general ways to do this that you are normally concerned with:

```
globalVar          = 12;
var globalVar2      = 13;              //using var may create a problem
window.globalVar3   = 14;
```

These all essentially assign these variable names to the global object, but they are handled a little differently. This is usually not a problem until it comes time to remove them. One way is to assign them the value of `null`, similar to:

```
globalVar  = null;
globalVar2 = null;
globalVar3 = null;
```

This sets all three variables to `null` and will free up memory, but since they are in the global context they will not be completely removed by garbage collection. Another method for removing these variables is to use the `delete` method, similar to:

```
delete globalVar;
delete globalVar2;
delete globalVar3;
```

The `delete` method will normally completely remove the object. However, the global object declared with `var` (`globalVar2`) will not be removed and will still contain its value. When you try to access these variables now, accessing `globalVar` or `globalVar3` will throw a JavaScript error. Accessing `globalVar2` still shows the original value of 13;

Use of *undefined* variable

Be careful testing against `undefined` as a user can actually change the value of this variable and your tests may fail. I think this is highly unlikely and very easy to spot and correct. I assume that your content is all "trusted" content—that is, it has been reviewed by someone and does not contain malicious code. If you are coding in an environment where you may not have control over code that is added, then you may have to take that into account when deciding how to test variables. You would also have to add a lot more error checking in this instance.

Comparisons with == or ===

JavaScript has two equality operators that can be used to compare variables and constants.

Operator	Result
`==` type-converting equality	JavaScript will attempt to coerce the variables to the same type and then compare them to see if they are equal
`===` strict equality	Variables must be same type and have same value to be considered equal

A few points about these operators:

- Expressions comparing objects are only true if they are comparing the same object.
- Null and undefined are considered the same if using ==, but not if using ===.
- As shown below, the speed performance of both operators is essentially the same.

The use of == to compare values can sometimes be OK if you know what you are doing. Using the strict compare === will ensure that the values are equal both in type and value but there may be times that the regular compare would be sufficient. Some places you need to be careful include:

- Reading values from cookies or similar storage. These normally will be internally represented as strings and the normal coercion may not work. You will have to force the numeric value you read in to be a number using something like a `parseInt`.
- If you are careful, you can use the coercing compare to make short compare statements. This is discussed in more detail in the section about testing for falsey values.

* Note. `switch` statements use strict equality comparisons by default. You need to be careful when substituting switch statements with regular `if` statements.

Declarations for the following tests for equality were:

```
var varA = 9;
var varB = "9";
var varC = "abc";
```

⏲ PERFORMANCE TESTING	OPS (bigger is better)		
	Safari	Chrome	Firefox
1. if (varA === 9)	1,555	605	1,042
2. if (varA == 9)	1,560	604	1,042
3. newA = parseInt(varB); if (newA === 9)	35	63	41
4. if (varB == 9)	40	30	23
5. if (varA == "9")	38	30	22
6. if (varC === "abc")	1,579	597	1,051
7. if (varC == "abc")	1,542	605	1,045

Test 3-1: http://www.nativeJavascript.com/tests/Test-Comparisons.html

These test cases analyze comparisons between strings and numbers where you have specific values you are testing and you know the type of each variable. The next section analyzes comparisons that are just plain true or false tests (falsey). The results of the above testing points to a few recommendations. The Safari browser appears to be optimized for some of these comparisons.

* Tests 1 and 2. If you are comparing two numbers that you know are numbers, both methods (== and ===) have the same performance. You can use the strict operator for consistency here.

* Tests 3, 4 and 5. If you are comparing a number that might be a string, either converting to a number before comparing, or allowing JavaScript to coerce the string to a number or a number to a string resulted in awful performance compared to the other tests.

* Test 6 and 7. The string to string comparison performance was essentially the same as the number to number compare.

Using the *typeof* command

JavaScript provides the `typeof` operator to determine the internal type of a variable. A common usage of this command would look like:

```
if (typeof idx == 'undefined') {
if (typeof(idx) == 'undefined') {     //you can add parens if you want
```

Since `typeof` is an operator and not a method you do not need parentheses around the variable. The values returned by using the `typeof` command are shown in the following table.

Variable Type	typeof Result
not declared	"undefined"
undefined	"undefined"
null	"object"
boolean	"boolean"
number	"number"
string	"string"
array	"object"
date	"object"
function	"function"
any other object	"object"

You can use the *typeof* operator to test for the type or existence of JavaScript variables. The rules to keep in mind when declaring and testing variables include:

1. If you have not declared a variable and attempt to reference it in a statement, you will get a JavaScript error that essentially stops execution. The only operation you can perform that won't produce this error is a `typeof` operation, or using something like `window.x` where x is the variable name.

2. Variables can be declared first with a var statement, or passed in as an argument to a function.

3. Variables that have been declared but not set to a value will return a typeof value of "undefined".

4. It is an expensive and usually unnecessary operation to use typeof to test for the existence of variables before referencing them. Normally, you should know from your code if variables have been declared and what type they are before using them. As the following tests show, a test for a variable that may not be declared yet is almost 300 times slower than just checking for a variable being undefined. If you just can't be sure, then go ahead and declare the variable in the correct context at the start of your code and set it to some obvious error value that you will check later. If you can't be sure of the variable's existence, then be sure to test first with `typeof`.

The following tests were done by using different methods to test for the existence or value of variables. You can see how slow the test for a variable that has not been declared yet is. The declarations before the tests were run were:

```
//varA not declared
var varB = 1;
var varC;
var varD = null;
var obj2 = {};
```

🏎️ **PERFORMANCE TESTING**		**OPS** (bigger is better)		
		Safari	Chrome	Firefox
1. `if (typeof varA == "undefined")` `//true`		393	2	348
2. `if (typeof varA === "undefined")` `//true`		385	2	350
3. `if (window.varA == undefined)` `//true`		87	1	1
4. `if (window.varA === undefined)` `//true`		389	1	1
5. `if (typeof varB == "undefined")` `//false`		1,532	626	56
6. `if (typeof varC == "undefined")` `//true`		1,549	630	1,043
7. `if (varC == undefined)` `//true`		113	620	1,042
8. `if (typeof varD == "undefined")` `//false`		1,542	627	35
9. `if (varD == undefined)` `//true`		118	629	1,045
10 `if (obj2.b == undefined)` `//true`		97	633	1,045

Test 3-2: http://www.nativeJavascript.com/tests/Test-CompareUndefined.html

A few things to note about the results in the above table:

- All of the methods that tested for the existence of `varA` (which was never declared) were slow. That is more reason to write your code so that step is not necessary. Testing for a variable that does not exist forces the browser to spend more time looking.

- Using a test like `window.varA` to test for the existence is often slower than using `typeof`.

- The use of `===` to test equality performed essentially the same as `==`. The other tests that used `===` were not shown as the numbers were the same.

- Most of the other comparisons were essentially equally efficient, except for Safari when testing against the constant undefined in tests 7 and 9.

- The tests for variable `varD` (tests 8 and 9) involved testing a `null` value. `Null` is considered an object which is why method 8 returned false as the `typeof` would have returned "object". The speeds in Chrome were the same but Firefox and Safari had mixed results.

- The tests in methods 7 and 9 return true for both undefined variables (but declared) and variables set to `null`, and they ran at about equal speeds.

- You can test for the existence of properties on objects without using `typeof`, as method 10 shows. In order for this to work, however, the object must exist or this will throw an error. This is why the test for `window.varA` works. This was much slower on Safari.

Testing for '*falsey*' values

Testing for "*falsey*" values means testing variables by relying on JavaScript's loose typing rules to determine if variables match your rules. Be careful using this method and fully understand what represents a "false" value in these comparisons. For the purpose of this comparison, the following values are considered to be "false". Any other value would be considered "true".

falsey values considered false
- false
- undefined
- null
- NaN
- 0 (but not "0")
- ""

Using this type of test normally means you are using the loose equality operator (==) as it does not care about the initial type of each item compared. You can see the previous section for details about comparing actual values. This section just covers the check for truthy or falsey equality. The main uses of this type of test include:

- **If statements.** You can use something simple like: `if (varA) {`
- **Function arguments.** You can make sure you have valid arguments using code like the following. Here, if `varA` evaluates to false, the default value will be used for `varA`.
  ```
  function (varA) {
      varA = varA || "default";
  ```
- **Return values.** You can use something like the following to return values from your functions:
  ```
  return varA || "default";
  ```

All tests in the table below returned a value of *true*. Declarations for the following tests for equality were as follows.

```
var varA;
var varB = null;
var varC = 0;
var varD = "";
var varE = false;
```

PERFORMANCE TESTING	OPS (bigger is better)		
	Safari	Chrome	Firefox
1. if (!varA)	697	612	1,048
2. if (varA == undefined)	116	613	1,023
3. if (!varB)	1,557	613	1,010
4. if (varB == null)	1,553	580	1,032
5. if (!varC)	1,560	604	1,013
6. if (varC == 0)	1,535	592	1,038
7. if (!varD)	1,557	606	1,051
8. if (varD == "")	1,571	600	1,019
9. if (!varE)	1,571	591	1,048
10. if (varE == false)	1,575	605	1,016
11. if (varB == false || varB == undefined || varB == null)	120	600	1,032
12. if (varB == null || varB == false || varB == undefined)	1,567	592	1,038

Test 3-3: http://www.nativeJavascript.com/tests/Test-FalseyCompare.html

These test cases were fairly consistent:

- Most of the time the simpler `if (!varA)` performs as well as using a compound statement that tests all possible types, except on Safari. This can be true if your compound statement does not match on the first test. In tests 11 and 12, test 11 used to be much slower because it had to test all 3 conditions before it matched. But now, it is almost the same except on Safari. It can't hurt to list multiple tests in the order you think will result in the most common tests first.

- ◆ Be careful if you are using a falsey test to determine if a variable has been set, but valid values for the variable include 0 (zero) or an empty string. Those will equate to false but the variable has really been set.

Short-circuiting if statements

If statements that test multiple conditions are subject to *short-circuiting* which means that the statement will exit as soon as it can determine its truthfulness. Tests 11 and 12 in the previous test are examples of this. In the following statement using the && (and) operator, if isValid is false, the second test for age is never carried out:

```
if (isValid && age == 12) {}
```

Likewise, in the following statement using || (or), if x is null, then the second test is not done.

```
if (x == null || y == null) {}
```

Besides trying to put the most likely tests first, you can also use this behavior to avoid errors caused by undefined values. If you are not sure of whether a test will throw an error, you can test for the existence of items before trying to examine their properties. Forgetting to do this is a frequent cause of errors that may not be caught until you test all corner cases of possible values that are compared.

```
var a = null;
var b = [3, 2, 3];
if (a.length > 0) {}        //this throws an error
if (b.length > 0) {}        //OK  -is true
if (a && a.length > 0) {} //OK - is false
```

Avoid assignment mistakes in *if* statements

A common mistake in JavaScript conditional statements is to forget to use two or three = signs and instead just use one. This is a valid statement so JavaScript will normally run it. It might look like:

```
if (x = 5) {
```

instead of

```
if (x == 5) {
```

Some compilers, SDK's, or programs like JSLint will notify you of this kind of problem. A method that some programmers use is often called the *Yoda* method. As Yoda might describe your comparison statement as "if 5 is your variable x", you write:

```
if (5 == x) {
```

Written in that order, if you make a mistake and write if (5 = x), it will cause an obvious JavaScript error right away, instead of introducing a subtle bug that may be hard to find. Use it if you are comfortable with it and helps you write better code. Personally, I find the syntax confusing and rely on JSLint to find any mistakes.

Creating new arrays and objects

There are two main ways to create native arrays and objects in JavaScript (not counting methods like split or object constructors). You will see examples of both methods everywhere. The more traditional methods is:

```
var a = new Array();
var b = new Object();
```

You can also use the following shortcut methods:

```
var a = [];
var b = {};
```

As the following table points out, you really should use the second method as there are some huge increases in performance on some browsers.

	PERFORMANCE TESTING	OPS (bigger is better)		
		Safari	Chrome	Firefox
1. var a = new Array();		1,521	69	972
2. var a = [];		1,501	181	958
3. var a = new Object();		1,468	29	5
4. var a = {};		1,481	99	1,001

Test 3-4: http://www.nativeJavascript.com/tests/Test-CreateObjects.html

There are a few important points that are highlighted by these results.

- The Safari browser seems to be optimized to treat all methods approximately the same though the shorthand method is still faster.

- Chrome was slower for all methods but the shorthand method is still much faster.

- The long method for object creation on Firefox was incredibly slow for some reason. Use the shorthand method.

Hoisting

JavaScript uses a method called "hoisting" to effectively move all variable declarations to the top of the enclosing code, such as the module or function. Only the declaration will be hoisted but not the assignment value.

```
console.log("varA value = " + varA);
var varA = "newvalue";
```

This will display the following on the console log:

```
varA value = undefined
```

It displays "undefined" because the declaration was hoisted but the variable value was not set yet. The same applies if you are using the variable assignment method to declare functions, similar to:

```
var parseData = function() {};
```

In this case, the function parseData will be declared and hoisted, but it will not be available to be called until code after its declaration.

If you declare the same function in the following way, it will be available anywhere in the current scope, above or below:

```
function parseData() {}
```

This is another reason that you should put all your variable declarations at the top of each closure to ensure your logic won't be misinterpreted.

Another use of assigning a function to a variable (even though it won't get hoisted) is that you can assign similar functions to elements of an array. Rather than have one function with conditional logic to handle different variations like sort order, you can assign the optimized version of each function to an array element, and then call the proper function using an index, such as:

```
var dateFunctions   = [];
dateFunctions[0]    = function() {
  //code for first date function
};
dateFunctions[1] = function() {
  //code for second date function
};
dateFunctions[1]();              //call second function
```

Converting strings to numbers

There are times that you need to force a string variable to be treated as a number. This will be required if you are using the strict equality operator (===) for comparisons or if the value is used as part of a formula or an index into an array. Sometimes values retrieved from cookies or similar storage appear to be numbers but are represented internally as strings and have to be forced to numbers. There are several ways to make this conversion.

- **parseInt():** Converts a valid string to an integer number. Be sure to add the radix at the end of the operation to avoid certain strings being converted to a base other than base10. Strings starting with a zero "0" will default to octal (base 8) if you don't specify the base. The command should look like: `var x = parseInt("342", 10);`
- **Number():** Converts a valid string to a number.
- **parseFloat():** Converts a valid string to a floating point number including the decimal if any.
- **Math.floor():** Rounds a number or valid string by rounding down.
- **Math.ceil():** Rounds a number or valid string by rounding up.
- **Math.round():** Rounds a number or valid string to the closest integer. If the decimal portion is equal to .5 or greater, it is rounded up; otherwise, it is rounded down.
- **subtract 0** (-0): Having a - 0 operation at the end of a string will force it to a number.

Value	parseInt	Number	parseFloat	Math.floor	Math.ceil	Math.round	- 0
Actual value returned by operation							
true	NaN	1	NaN	1	1	1	1
Date	NaN	138...	NaN	138...	138...	138...	138...
"123"	123	123	123	123	123	123	123
"122.23"	122	122.23	122.23	122	123	122	122.23
"322 333"	322	NaN	322	NaN	NaN	NaN	NaN
"abc123"	NaN	NaN	NaN	NaN	NaN	NaN	NaN
"123abc"	123	NaN	123	NaN	NaN	NaN	NaN
"55.7"	55	55.7	55.7	55	56	56	55.7
"55.2"	55	55.2	55.2	55	56	55	55.2
"123,456"	123	NaN	123	NaN	NaN	NaN	NaN
Relative number of operations (bigger is better)							
Chrome	401	1,270	404	895	1,191	827	4,458
Safari	928	1,400	880	1,761	1,780	1,492	1,610
Firefox	127	1,437	119	1,409	1,409	1,382	1,085

Test 3-5: http://www.nativeJavascript.com/tests/Test-StringToNumber.html

Note: the cells indicating the date as "138..." were truncated for the display. The numbers returned were the full correct ms of the date objects, except where noted as returning NaN.

The last 3 rows show the relative number of operations per second for each browser to run each operation on all values. There are a few items to consider from this table:

- The two slowest operations were parseInt and parseFloat. These were anywhere from 1/10 to 1/2 the speed of the other operations, depending on the browser. parseInt on Firefox was really slow.

- If you are concerned with rounding, you will have to examine the results of the various operations to determine which type of rounding you need for your application.

- Strings with leading non-numeric characters were converted to NaN for all operations. Numbers formatted with commas returned incorrect values in all cases.

- If you expect your strings may have numbers followed by non-numeric characters, you will need to use the parseInt or parseFloat operations, or may want to use a regex operation like /^\d+/

- Chrome has super-optimized using -0 to convert the string. It is four times as fast as the other methods.

You have to be careful if you are using the addition operator (+) to combine literals or variables that might be a mixture of numeric and non-numeric characters. These operators will act as mathematical additions as long as the variables are numbers. As soon as a variable is detected to be a string, then that and all future operations in the same formula will act as string concatenations. See the following for examples of what happens.

Concatenating numbers and strings

```
var varA = "123";
var varB = varA + 4;
console.log(varB);              //displays 1234

var varC = +varA;
var varD = varC + 4;
console.log(varD);              //displays 127 since +varA forces varA
                               //to a number

var varE = "123" - 0;
var varF = varE + 4;
console.log(varF);              //displays 127 since the -0 forces varE
                               //to a number

var varG = 4 + 4 + "60" + 3;
console.log(varG);             //displays 8603

var varH = "123" + 4 + 5;
console.log(varH);              //displays 12345

var varJ = "123" + 4 + 5 + "789";
console.log(varJ);             //displays 12345789
```

Converting numbers to strings

Converting numbers to strings is much easier than the other way around but you still have a few options to consider. You can:

- Simply add a string or null string ("") to the number, similar to:
```
var num    = 22;
var numStr = num + "";                  //numStr is now a string
```

- Use the toString() method to force it to a string. This has the added benefit of allowing you to specify the number's base for the conversion.
```
var num    = 22;
var numStr = num.toString();            //uses default base of 10
var newStr = (32767).toString(16);      //produces "7fff"
```

- Use the toFixed() method if you want to control the number of decimal places, or even add decimal places. This might come in handy if you are trying to line up decimal numbers in a table. If the command has to round the last decimal place, you may get different rounding results based on your browser so you should test this if it is important. Just remember that the result is a string so don't try to do math on it.
```
var num     = 8.3;
var newStr  = num.toFixed(2);       // "8.30"
var newNum  = newStr + 1.1;         // "8.301.1"  Oops!
var newNum2 = (num + 1.1).toFixed(2)  // "9.40"   Correct!
```

The declaration for the following tests for converting was:
```
var num = 22.5;
```

⏱ PERFORMANCE TESTING	OPS (bigger is better)		
	Safari	Chrome	Firefox
1. `var numStr = num + "";`	33	607	1,038
2. `var numStr = num.toString();`	16	39	64
3. `var numStr = num.toString(10);`	15	24	55
4. `var numStr = num.toFixed(1);`	7	3	9
5. `var numStr = ((parseInt(num * 10)) / 10) + "";`	20	54	35

Test 3-6: http://www.nativeJavascript.com/tests/Test-NumberToString.html

You can see from the performance numbers that the simple operation of adding a null string was faster in every case, up to 20 times faster in Chrome and Firefox. The `toFixed` option was very, very slow but if you need it, you will have to use it. Test 5 showed another way to convert a number to a string with one decimal place. It is several times faster than `toFixed`.

Be careful of floating point arithmetic

JavaScript stores all numbers as double precision floating point numbers, using 64 bits to store each number. This can cause precision errors if you are not careful. Note the following expression:

```
var x = .2 + .1;                    //x = 0.30000000000000004
```

If you need better precision in these cases, you may need to multiply and divide the numbers, doing something similar to:

```
var x = ((.2 * 10) + (.1 * 10)) / 10;    //x = 0.3
```

Other random bits about numbers

There are a few other possible pitfalls concerning the use of numbers in JavaScript including:

- **Leading zeroes.** Some browsers will interpret a number that has a leading zero as an octal number. Thus,
  ```
  var x = 012;                //x = 10 (octal 012 = decimal 10)
  var x = 12;                 //x = 12
  ```
- **Hexadecimal.** To set a number using a hexadecimal representation, simply precede the number with 0x, similar to:
  ```
  var x = 0x12;               //x = 18 (hexadecimal 12 = decimal 18)
  ```
- To produce the hexadecimal representation of this number, you can use the `toString` method with the base number in parenthesis, similar to:
  ```
  var str = x.toString(16); //str = "12" (hex (base 16) of decimal 18)
  ```
- **Infinity.** You can set a variable to a value of Infinity by using the keyword `Infinity`, or by dividing by zero. Thus,
  ```
  var x = Infinity;         //x is now larger than all other numbers
  ```
- **NaN.** This represents "Not A Number". Variables can be set to this value due to a bad math operation such as dividing by a string, or doing a parseInt type operation on a string that can't be coerced to a number. You can use the built-in isNaN() function to determine if a variable is a number before using it, similar to:
  ```
  if (!isNaN(x)) y = x / 10;
  ```

Loops

There are a number of ways to handle loops in JavaScript. You should understand the relative performance of each and ways to optimize the performance when you use them. Obviously, if you are just looping through a few items, you don't have to worry about performance. But a lot of the code I have written has dealt with thousands or tens of thousands of items, and performance is of concern. I think it is always a good idea to just learn the best way to write the loops and use that all the time. I don't think any of these suggestions detracts from the code readability, with the possible exception of having the loop count backwards. This used to have a performance advantage which has mostly gone away. Using local variables is often the best way to improve your loop's performance. Methods vary whether you are looping through arrays or objects, and that may influence your decision to use arrays or objects.

The main methods to use are:

- `for` loop: This is the most common method and looks like:

  ```
  for (var i=0; i < newlen; i++) {}
  ```

- `while` loop: Similar to the for loop:

  ```
  while (i < newlen) { i++;}
  ```

- `do` loop: Similar to while except it will always execute at least once.

  ```
  do { i++; } while (i < newlen);
  ```

- `forEach` loop: A special JavaScript operation that runs your supplied function on each element in the array.

  ```
  arr.forEach(function (val){
    var y = val;
  })
  ```

- `for...in` loop: This is mainly used to iterate over properties of objects but is very slow however you use it. This is mainly due to the fact this operation is not optimized by browsers.

  ```
  for (var name in obj) {
    var val = obj[name];
  }
  ```

- `for ...in loop` checking `hasOwnProperty`: If you are unsure if other properties have been added to the object prototype for the object you are checking, you should also add a check for that using the `hasOwnProperty` method.

  ```
  for (var name in obj) {
    if (obj.hasOwnProperty(name)) {
      var val = obj[name];
    }
  }
  ```

<table-icon> PERFORMANCE TESTING	OPS (bigger is better)		
	Safari	Chrome	Firefox
1. for (i=0; i < newArr.length; i++)	68	39	4
2. for (var i=0; i < newArr.length; i++)	96	50	105
3. same as 2 but cache newArr.length	96	50	102
4. same as 3 but cache newArr to local array	290	75	157
5. same as 4 but count backwards	282	61	78
6. while (i—)	287	60	77
7. Duff's device - for loop with 8 statements	138	122	191
8. forEach with local copy of array	6	5	104
9. for (var name in object)	12	.3	.3
10. for (var name in object) w/hasOwnProperty	.4	.5	.2

Test 3-7: http://www.nativeJavascript.com/tests/Test-Loops.html

The relative results were fairly consistent across the browsers tested. The results point out a few important points to keep in mind when coding loops, particularly for large arrays. One of the main areas of optimization for your application will be loops that iterate over a large number of items. You should be able to use the optimizations pointed out here every time your write a loop so that you start with optimal code. Only later when you identify a particular loop as a continuing bottleneck would you consider something like the Duff's device solution.

- The performance increased from test 1 to test 4. This was due to using local variables declared with a `var` in the function instead of global variables. Besides making the variable `i` local, another gain was made by setting a local variable equal to the global array, and then using that value. This obviously may not apply to your code but keep it in mind.

- The JavaScript method `forEach` allows you to specify a function to perform on each array member but it is very slow. This test was using it only for a simple operation so your code may have uses that would benefit from using it.

- Using the `for (var name in object)` method was really slow. This shouldn't be used unless you have no other way to access the values. This is usually used for objects but is still slow. You could consider keeping the property names in an array and using that. This method causes the browser to skip optimization.

- The fastest way, except on Safari, was the "Duff's device". This method relies on reducing the overhead of all the loop iterations by placing more statements inside each loop iteration. The upside is a great increase in speed. The downside is that it is slightly harder to read the code and it increases the code size. The method tested above is shown below. The accepted method is to carry out eight (8) iterations inside each loop, after first reducing the number to an even multiple of eight.

Duff's Device Example

```
var y;
var locarr = newArr;
var nlen   = locarr.length;
var i      = 0;
var n      = nlen % 8;
while (n--) {
    y = locarr[i++];
}
n = parseInt(nlen/8);
while (n--) {
    y = locarr[i++];
    y = locarr[i++];
    y = locarr[i++];
    y = locarr[i++];
    y = locarr[i++];
    y = locarr[i++];
    y = locarr[i++];
    y = locarr[i++];
}
```

Removing functions no longer needed

Your code most likely will have functions or code that is executed only once when the application starts. You should arrange this code in a manner where it can be deleted after it is used so it can be cleared from memory. The easiest way is to simply set the function name to null, similar to:

```
function addData(){//code here}
addData();                        //called only one time
addData = null;
```

The `delete` command is really meant to be used for delete object properties, not functions and it works differently depending on how functions and variables are declared. The use of null will result in the function being removed during the next garbage collection. The use of strict mode affects which items you can delete as well.

Date objects are passed by reference

Date objects, as well as any other objects, are passed by reference, not value. You need to be careful if you are setting variables equal to existing date objects because they will be linked. If you want to create a unique new date object equal to the value of an existing date object, use code similar to:

```
var dateOne = new Date();                        //new date set to now
var dateTwo = dateOne;                           //date object linked
                                                 //to dateOne
var dateThree = new Date(dateOne.getTime()); //unique date set to value
                                                 //of dateOne but not linked
```

Concatenating strings

There may be cases where you have to create one large string by concatenating smaller strings. This is often used when creating HTML strings that will be used with an innerHTML property. There are several ways to accomplish string concatenation. The methods that are faster have larger memory requirements so you will have to decide on the proper trade off. Browsers have gotten much better in optimizing memory usage when concatenating and attempt to minimize the amount of copying memory blocks.

PERFORMANCE TESTING	OPS (bigger is better)		
	Safari	Chrome	Firefox
1. str = str.concat("abcd");	337	475	341
2. str+= "a" + "b" + "c" + "d";	383	988	700
3. array.push("abcd"); str = array.join("");	323	192	283
4. array[array.length]="abcd";str=array.join("");	323	188	301
5. str+="abcd"	786	982	814
6. str = str + "abcd"	823	979	838

Test 3-8: http://www.nativeJavascript.com/tests/Test-ConcatenateStrings.html

The methods were mainly consistent across browsers though there were some differences in the test results. There are a few lessons to be learned here.

- Using either str+= or str+str performed better than using arrays or .concat to add new text. However, if you look at the memory usage, the story is reversed. Granted, most of the extra memory used will be garbage collected but you really want to try to avoid creating garbage in the first place. Depending on the browser and the strings that are concatenated, you may see the memory usage using str+ or str+str double or more that using the arrays.

- You should also minimize the number of additive operations. On some browsers, it will be faster to add the string "abc" than to add "a" + "b" + "c".

Regular expressions

Regular expressions can work almost like magic to find or replace text in strings. Entire books have been written about the use of regular expressions, in programs ranging from Microsoft Word to JavaScript. I am not going to go into any detail about how to construct individual regular expressions since there are so many good resources. In general, you use them for finding or replacing specified string patterns inside other strings. You can use them to validate input fields like phone numbers or zip codes, or to filter text based on matching fields. They can be incredibly powerful but also incredibly confusing. If you choose to use them, make sure you comment your code so others will know what the expression is doing.

The general uses in JavaScript include the following methods:

- `exec`: searches a string for a match and returns an array of information.
- `test`: searches a string for a match and returns true if it is found.
- `match`: searches a string for a match and returns an array of information.
- `search`: searches a string for a match and returns the index of the match if found.
- `replace`: replaces occurrences of a matched string with another string.
- `split`: splits a string based on matched expression and returns an array.

There are some great test tools for testing your regular expressions as you figure out the optimal method to use. I use `http://www.regexpal.com/`

Should I switch to using *switch*?

There are several ways to set up your logic statements to compare values. Each one has its strengths and best uses. The four main methods are:

- object property:
  ```
  obj = {};
  obj["a"] = 4;
  newVar = (obj[x]) ? obj[x] : 5;
  ```
- switch statement:
  ```
  switch(x) {
      case "a":
          newVar = 4;
          break;
      default:
          newVar = 5;
  }
  ```
- ternary compare:
  ```
  newVar = (x == "a") ? 4 : 5;
  ```
- if statement:
  ```
  if (x == "a") {
      newVar = 4;
  } else {
      newVar = 5;
  }
  ```

PERFORMANCE TESTING	OPS (bigger is better)		
	Safari	Chrome	Firefox
1. x = obj[varA];	52	434	346
2. switch(varA) {	1,567	521	1,048
3. x = (varA == "d") ? 1 : 2;	1,557	497	1,035
4. if (varA == "d") {	1,579	502	1,058

Test 3-9: http://www.nativeJavascript.com/tests/Test-IfOrCase.html

I carried out several tests with these different operators. The results above were for testing for four different variables and where the correct variable was the second one tested. The results were scattered, but there are some general lessons we can learn.

- For simple comparisons of just one or two cases, the ternary operator (test 3) is probably best. You can also link ternary compares together, such as:

```
newVar = (x == 1) ? 5 : (x == 2) ? 6 : 7;
```

- The object comparison was slower on all browsers.

- Your exact use would also dictate which method to use. If you have a large number of items to test for, the first option (using an object lookup) might be best. It would most likely be less code and easier to read and maintain, but it is very slow. You should test the method using your actual data.

- Other methods to optimize the performance include breaking the tests down into groups and then testing the subgroup that matches. Thus, if you had to test for each number between 1 and 100, you might have the first test be for groups of ten, such as x < 10, x < 20, etc. Then, within each of those groups, you would test for the specific number.

Note. `switch` statements use strict equality comparisons by default. You need to be careful when substituting switch statements with regular if statements.

Testing arguments passed to a function

You might be passing arguments to a function that might be called by existing code that doesn't include the new arguments. JavaScript doesn't require the number of arguments in the calling statement to agree with the number declared in the function statement (some IDEs may flag this condition.) So try to add your new arguments so that the `false` (or `undefined`) condition is the default condition. Thus, if the calling statement doesn't include the argument, you can treat it the same as including a false or null object. Another method you should try to always use is to check for arguments and supply a default value if the argument is not included or is undefined. In the following code, the default value will be used if the argument is equal to: "", 0, null, or undefined so this wouldn't work if 0 or "" were valid values. The function would look something like:

```
function thisFunction(arg1,arg2) {
    arg1 = arg1 || 1;              //default is 1
    arg2 = arg2 || "default";      //default is "default"
}
```

setTimeout is your friend

There are two methods that allow you to defer execution of your code to a later time. Since JavaScript is single-threaded these methods also allow you to have some control over the order of code execution. The methods are:

- `setTimeout()`: This allows you to execute a specified function or code snippet in a specified number of milliseconds (ms). This will run the specified code one time. There is a corresponding `clearTimeout()` used to clear an existing timer.

- `setInterval()`: This acts similar to `setTimeout` but the referenced code will keep running every xx milliseconds until you issue a `clearInterval()` command. When you execute this command, the first instance will not be triggered until the specified time interval. You are not guaranteed that your function will even fire at every interval since other operations may block their execution.

There are several ways to set timeouts. Variations cover how the function part of the operation is set. You may see the following methods. These apply for both `setTimeout` and `setInterval`.

- `setTimeout("doFunc",100)`; has to do eval which is costly and could cause problems.

- `setTimeout(doFunc,100)`; this will call the doFunc function in 100ms but you can't pass in arguments.

- `setTimeout(function(){doFunc(varA);},100)`; This is the best way to set your timeouts and intervals as it avoids evals and allows you to pass arguments directly into your function.

There are many ways that timers can help your code. Be sure you are familiar with all of them. Remember that there is no guarantee that your timers will fire at exactly the time you specify. The CPU has to finish its current thread before it can handle the timer function. And you should remember to stop timers that are no longer needed using the `clearTimeout` and `clearInterval` commands.

- Timeout zero (0). I use this all the time and you will find lots of uses. The main use is to stop your processing to allow another process to run. You don't even need a number; zero will suffice. The most common uses are:
  - **Screen update.** The timeout will allow the screen to update if required. You might have made DOM objects using `innerHTML` and they haven't been created yet so you can set a timeout which will allow the elements to be created.
  - **Split up long processes.** You shouldn't have functions that take a long time to execute without releasing control. You can break up these long functions into two or more functions and use `setTimeout(xx,0)` to relinquish the processor in between.
  - **Process events.** You may need to allow keyboard, mouse, or touch events to be processed. These events will be queued up until the processor frees up to accept them.

- Wait until code is loaded or an event happens. You can use a `setTimeout` at the start of a function to allow code execution to wait until a certain event happens, such as:

```
function thisFunction() {
    clearTimeout(loadTimer);
    if (!filesLoaded) {          //test for some external condition
        loadTimer = setTimeout(function(){thisFunction();},200);
        return;
    }
    //rest of function
```

- Fallback in case data load fails. You can have your `xmlHTTP` requests handle timeouts or you can also add your own timeout that will run in case the data never loads. You would need to place a `clearTimeout` call in the callback code that normally runs when the data loads.

- Minute timers. The best way to handle screen designs that display the current time every minute is to set up a master timer routine that gets fired every minute and updates all routines that have registered a callback for the event. The routine updates a variable, updates the views, and then issues a new timeout call for the next minute. Creating new Date objects is a little slow and most of the time you only need a date object that is accurate to the closest minute, so this is a good way to always have a valid date object.

```
function minuteTimer() {
    clearTimeout(minuteTimeout);
    globalDate        = new Date();
    globalDisplayDate = dFormat(globalDate);
    //update your views here if they have registered a listener
    //run again in one minute on the minute
    var nsecs = (60 - globalDate.getSeconds()) * 1000;
    minuteTimeout = setTimeout(function(){minuteTimer();},nsecs);
}
```

Reduce the creation of garbage

The term "garbage" in JavaScript refers to memory once used for variables, objects, or functions that has been freed up because it is no longer referenced by anything. There is no way to force this garbage to be collected. Each browser has its own mechanism of determining when garbage should be collected and freed. With efficient collection and larger memory sizes, the issue is not as critical as before, but you should still strive to minimize the creation of garbage. I have programmed high performance scrolling applications that would be adversely affected by a sudden garbage collection carried out by the browser. The two issues you should always keep in mind are:

- **Free up unused memory.** Any variables that leave scope will be garbage collected. This includes local variables declared with a var statement inside a function. Once the function exits, those items will be de-referenced and available for collection. But other functions or variables in the global space will stay referenced until you delete them or set them to null. Be careful of any variables that stay referenced because of closures.

- **Don't make garbage in the first place.** Make your loops as tight as possible and try to avoid creating a lot of temporary strings. Make your data structures compact and try to minimize the amount of fetched data you must throw away. I was able to take what would have been 168MB of data downloaded from the server and creating garbage and create a small 3MB file that was all JSON data.

Just a simple change to use integers instead of strings inside loops can save memory. Reuse of integers uses less memory than using strings. Instead of something like:

```
var varNew = ((i%3)==0) ? "on" : "off";
```

just use:

```
var varNew = ((i%3)==0) ? 1 : 0;
```

Lookup of arrays vs. objects

There are instances where an array makes the most sense for storing your data and other times an object or array of objects makes more sense. You need to decide which is the optimal method for your usage. The main factors to consider are:

- **Method of access.** How will you access the data? Do you need to have a named property to identify the member, or will an integer index suffice? Will the items need to be ordered?

- **Performance.** How often will the data be accessed? Will speed of access be important?

- **Memory.** How large a data set will you be handling? How important will memory usage be to your application?

- **Number of properties.** Objects or arrays with more properties tend to take longer to access than those with fewer properties though this is hard to compare.

- **Readability.** What ever method you select, you need to make sure that your code remains readable and you properly document the usage.

PERFORMANCE TESTING	OPS (bigger is better)		
	Safari	Chrome	Firefox
1. Object(20 properties): x = obj20[i]["9"];	9	20	100
2. Array(20 properties): x = arr20[i][8];	350	360	270
3. Object(10 properties): x = obj10[i]["4"];	9	30	150
4. Object(3 properties): x = obj3[i]["1"];	9	30	180
5. Array(10 properties): x = arr10[i][3];	360	360	320
6. Array(3 properties): x = arr3[i][0];	430	370	340

Test 3-10: http://www.nativeJavascript.com/tests/Test-ArraysOrObjects.html

The main result from these tests is that arrays are always faster to access than objects. However, your application may have values and methods of filling in the properties that are different from the tests I used, so you should carefully analyze your application.

- The Safari and Chrome browsers handled array lookups much faster (12-40 times) no matter how many properties were tested.

- Firefox had faster access times with arrays, but the difference between its array and object access was much smaller than the other browsers.

- If you have to create the object property name by concatenating strings, such as newObj["a"+i], the performance really falls off.

- The object lookups had similar performance whether you use the format newObj.prop or newObj["prop"].

Memory Use. Browsers have made some improvements here with storing objects vs. arrays. There is either little difference or objects actually can take up less memory but this is highly dependent on your data structure and actual data stored. You need to test your own data structure if you are concerned about memory usage. Minimize the number and size of properties wherever you can. If memory usage is more critical than performance, you can even store one comma delimited string containing multiple properties, but you will suffer a significant performance loss when accessing the information. You have to decide what trade-off to make. Perhaps you need to store a lot of data but only infrequently access it, so the latter method makes sense, or store the data as bits as discussed in the next section.

Using different values for True/False including bitwise operations

We had looked earlier at speed differences using falsey comparisons on values like true/false or 0/1. You often have properties on objects or arrays that are used essentially as flags having only two states. You can use either true/false or 1/0 in these cases.

You may also have collections that have a number of true/false flags on the same object. You can combine them into one integer value to save memory without sacrificing performance. Each bit in the number can represent a true/false value.

To Set:

```
var filt = 0;
filt |= 1;      //1st bit on      - filt equal to 1
filt |= 4;      //3rd bit on      - filt equal to 5
filt |= 32;     //6th bit also on - filt now equal to 37
```

To Test:

To test if a specific bit is on, even if other bits are on:

```
if (filt&32) ...         //true
if (filt&4) ...          //true
```

Using Math.pow to set values:

Normally this method of storage will map to some list of variables or perhaps an index into an array. Thus, we want to have an easy way to set and get a specific value, let's say bit 6. The best way to do this is to use the built-in function `Math.pow()` and raising the number two (2) to the power of your index, starting at zero (0). The setting method described above would look like:

```
var filt = 0;
filt |= Math.pow(2, 0);      //1st bit on - (use 0 for 1st bit)
filt |= Math.pow(2, 2);      //3rd bit on - (use 2 for 3rd bit)
filt |= Math.pow(2, 5);      //6th bit on - (use 5 for 6th bit)
```

⏱ PERFORMANCE TESTING	OPS (bigger is better)		
	Safari	Chrome	Firefox
1. Test using bitwise property &1 or &2	156	102	156
2. Test with property = 1 or 0	156	102	154
3. Test with property = true or false	157	51	156

Test 3-11: http://www.nativeJavascript.com/tests/Test-Bitwise.html

Remember that in addition to getting some performance gains, the main saving will most likely be storage space and bandwidth if the data is requested from a server. Reducing the number of object or array properties can be significant. This is a good case where the change improves both memory and performance—just make sure you comment the code to indicate what you are doing.

Sparse arrays

A sparse array is a numerical array whose members are not consecutive, or worded another way, has a number of identical values of `undefined`. If the array is too sparse, it essentially turns into a lookup object. You can create this array by assigning values to elements that are not sequential in a number of ways, similar to:

```
var newArr  = [];
newArr[0]   = "one";
newArr[330] = "thirty-three";
```

⏲ PERFORMANCE TESTING	OPS (bigger is better)		
	Safari	Chrome	Firefox
1. Sparse array - every 50th element	233	310	82
2. Regular array - all 0-10000 elements	5,050	3,744	4,993

Test 3-12: http://www.nativeJavascript.com/tests/Test-SparseArray.html

The above tests show how slow accessing a sparse array can be compared to a regular array, up to 50 times slower. By making the array sparse, it can make lookup times slower. However, the performance varies with browsers and with how sparse the array is. You can have arrays that have sparseness that are not slow. In general, if you are using an array for data that turns out to be too sparse, you should consider using an object with properties instead.

Populating arrays

Arrays can be populated in three main ways (they can also be created by other methods such as `str.split()`). You can use the push method to add a new element to the end of the array, or use an assignment operation to assign the new value to a specific array item.

⏲ PERFORMANCE TESTING	OPS (bigger is better)		
	Safari	Chrome	Firefox
1. newArr.push("abc" + i);	1,322	3,891	1,588
2. newArr[newArr.length] = "abc" + i;	1,288	4,000	1,749
3. newArr[i] = "abc" + i;	1,303	3,963	1,637
4. Duffs: newArr[i+n] = five at a time	1,296	4,156	1,671

Test 3-13: http://www.nativeJavascript.com/tests/Test-PopulatingArrays.html

The performance of these measures has varied from the previous browser versions. Now there is not much difference at all. If you have large arrays and performance is an issue, the fastest method was usually something like the Duff's device discussed earlier. This limits the number of loop iterations if you are able to incorporate this in your code. Something like the following (which is a variation of Duff's device) might work for your application but may not be worth it):

```
var duffArray = [];
for (var i=0; i < 10000; i+=5) {
  duffArray[i]   = "abc" + i;
  duffArray[i+1] = "abc" + (i+1);
  duffArray[i+2] = "abc" + (i+2);
  duffArray[i+3] = "abc" + (i+3);
  duffArray[i+4] = "abc" + (i+4);
}
```

Clearing arrays

Because arrays are passed by reference, you have to be careful when you create new arrays that reference existing arrays. Generally, changing values of the first array will also change the values when referencing the second array. Just be careful if you have to clear out the array. The following methods will give slightly different results:

```
array1 = [1, 2, 3];        //declare new array
array2 = array1;           //both arrays will have same values
```

Option 1 - set array1 to blank array

```
array1 = [];
Result:    //array1 = []
           //array2 = [1,2,3]
Setting it to null will have similar results.
```

Option 2 - setting length to zero

```
array1.length = 0;
Result:    //array1 = []
           //array2 = []
```

Option 3 - using splice

```
array1.splice(0,array1.length);
Result:    //array1 = []
           //array2 = []
```

Using 'pass by reference' to your advantage

In JavaScript, objects are passed by reference not by value. And since arrays are essentially objects, they inherit this same feature. I often use this to my advantage by setting temporary variables to objects and arrays that exist in more global contexts, and then use those variables to change values. Having a local reference to these objects makes the changes faster. In the following example, a global object and array are both changed inside a function, one by a passed in reference, the other by a temporary local variable. Both methods will work with objects or arrays.

```
object1 = {a: 1, b: 2, c: 3};
array1  = [1, 2, 3];
changeValues(object1);

function changeValues(obj) {
  obj.a         = 99;
  var temparray = array1;
  temparray[0]  = 88;
}
Result:    //object1.a = 99
           //array1[0] = 88
```

Handling typeahead

Typeahead refers to keys or events added to the event or key buffer because the user is pressing keys or buttons faster than the program can process them. Typeahead in input fields in usually handled differently and is acceptable most of the time. Handling the other kind of typeahead is sometimes desired and sometimes not. You should address it in your applications depending on your desired user experience. You normally want to allow one of several options:

- Go ahead and cache the events and carry out the operations in order. You will need to make each operation as fast as possible to try to keep up with the events.

- Carry out the first operation and discard all subsequent events or keystrokes until the operation finishes.

- Accept all the events or keystrokes but immediately enter a "fastmode" where you have a small, fast routine that can execute an operation fast enough to keep up with the events. This operation usually just shows a portion of the normal UI in order to be fast—this may be displaying just a channel number or page number but no data. You can use a timer that keeps getting cleared on each new event. Once there are no events within a certain time, the timer method will fire and you execute the main function which fills in all the screen.

The methods of either enabling or disabling your desired kind of typeahead handling include:

- **Disable element.** You can disable the button or element when it is pressed or touched the first time. You can do this in several ways including setting the `disabled` property to true. When the code that carries out the operation finishes, it will re-enable the element.

- **Use timeout.** You can use a timeout in the function that is called when the user presses the button. The timeout will call the actual function that carries out the operation.

```javascript
function handleKey() {
    clearTimeout(keyTimer);
    //code to display fast mode UI
    keyTimer = setTimeout(function(){fullDisplay();},220);
}
function fullDisplay() {
    //code to do full display
}
```

- **Timestamp.** Most browsers support a `timeStamp` property on the event. This can be used to essentially clear out the key or touch event buffer. This may be necessary if you have a function that runs for a long time and the user has been creating touch, mouse, or keyboard events. You can compare each event's `timeStamp` property to "now" and throw away keys that are older than a specified number of milliseconds, similar to:

```javascript
var now = new Date();
var diff = (now - event.timeStamp);
if (diff > 300) return;    //ignore keys from more than 300ms ago
```

Functions vs. inline code

You should always attempt to avoid long functions that might be hard to read and debug. This usually means structuring your code into files, objects, and functions to encapsulate the logic into smaller chunks. One time you may want to relax this rule is for performance reasons. If you have routines that have loops that execute the same code a large number of times, you may want to make all that code inline instead of in a function that is called from inside the loop. If you do call a function that is located in a different object, you may want to set a local reference to it outside the loop. You should always limit the creation of variables and objects inside loops and try to use integers instead of strings as much as possible. Loops can create a lot of garbage quickly so you want to reduce that as well.

Many browsers will optimize some functions depending on the code that is included. There are a number of constructs that will cause functions to not be optimized, such as `for-of` statements. Calling functions that contain the optimization killers will run much slower than the same code inline. These are shown by tests 3 and 4 below which use for `(var name in obj)`.

⏱ **PERFORMANCE TESTING**	**OPS** (bigger is better)		
	Safari	Chrome	Firefox
1. Function - optimized	91	62	78
2. Inline - optimized	91	62	80
3. Function - not optimized	22	7	14
4. Inline - not optimized	22	43	15

Test 3-14: http://www.nativeJavascript.com/tests/Test-InlineVsFunction.html

Try/Catch

The `try/catch` method enables you to have real error handling routines that will report on a variety of error conditions. You can also create your own error conditions by using `throw`. In the performance tests listed below, we tested two conditions each time—one when the try statement fails and throws an error, and the other time when it does not. We compared using a `try/catch` method with using a simple test for undefined. There is a performance penalty for using `try/catch` so you should only use it when you cannot control the error conditions that might arise, usually when importing or reading data. Compilers also will not optimize functions that contain `try/catch` statements. The tests that had conditions that failed the `try` step had extremely bad performance.

The simple try/catch statement used in our test looks like:

```
try {
  var a = newvar2;
}
catch (e) {
  var a = 2;
}
```

The statement we compared this to was:

```
var a = (typeof(newvar2) != "undefined") ? newvar2 : 2;
```

⏱	PERFORMANCE TESTING	OPS (bigger is better)		
		Safari	Chrome	Firefox
1. Inside try statement - fail		7	2	3
2. No try statement - fail		9,892	70	9,929
3. Inside try statement - pass		4,443	30,305	2,365
4. No try statement - pass		49,228	30,660	32,263

Test 3-15: http://www.nativeJavascript.com/tests/Test-TryCatch.html

Using fixed arrays

Using a regular array for 1,000,000 numbers takes up around 10,000,000 bytes or 10 bytes per element. JavaScript usually stores the numbers as 64-bit numbers and there are around 4 bytes per element overhead. However, there are special types of arrays that use a fixed number of bits for each element that might help you out. For example, if you can store your numbers in a `Int32Array`, you will reduce the memory usages to only 4,000,000 bytes. If you can use a 16-bit array, the usage goes down to 2,000,000 bytes. You will need to select the array type big enough to hold your expected values.

- Try to use integer arrays as much as possible. You often can use numbers instead of strings for many items, or even have a lookup table indexed by an integer.

- Use the smallest fixed array size possible. You will save a lot of memory and have better performance moving from 64 to 32 to 16 to 8 bits.

- Declare and allocate your fixed arrays once when your application starts.

- Use integer arrays as much as possible instead of float arrays. Depending on your range of values, you can multiply numbers by 10 or 100 to make them integers.

- Be aware of how floating point numbers are represented internally. This can cause computational errors. Just look at what the following simple loop produces:

```
for (var i=0; i < 1; i+=.1) {
    console.log(i);
}
0.1
0.2
0.3000000000000004
0.4
0.5
0.6
0.7
0.799999999999999
0.899999999999999
0.999999999999999
```

Types of fixed arrays

Name	Number of bytes	Type of number
Int8Array	1	8-bit signed integer
Uint8Array	1	8-bit unsigned integer
Uint8ClampedArray	1	8-bit unsigned integer (clamped)
Int16Array	2	16-bit signed integer
Uint16Array	2	16-bit unsigned integer
Int32Array	4	32-bit signed integer
Uint32Array	4	32-bit unsigned integer
Float32Array	4	32-bit floating point number
Float64Array	8	64-bit floating point number

Besides saving memory, fixed arrays can be populated faster on most browsers. It is a bit slower on Safari. There are so many variables involved including the size of the fixed array and what numbers you are adding that you should test your exact situation.

PERFORMANCE TESTING	OPS (bigger is better)		
	Safari	Chrome	Firefox
1. Populate regular array	13,981	3,947	6,182
2. Populate Int16Array	9,395	6,844	11,970

Test 3-16: http://www.nativeJavascript.com/tests/Test-FixedArray.html

Animation performance

Animating elements of your interface, besides looking cool, is often important in indicating what actions are taking place. You should use motion to emphasize what is happening - clicking a right arrow should slide in the next screen from the right, pressing a down arrow can slide the next page up from the bottom of the screen, etc. This is very important compared to just instantly displaying the new screen. However, animations can be costly in terms of performance. Try to avoid them if they are not needed and try to avoid animating multiple elements at the same time.

Image pre-caching

If you application uses images for your interface or to display as part of user selections, you may want to consider pre-caching them in order to speed up the display. This involves loading them before they are displayed and storing them in an `Image` object. Then, you can refer to this object when you want to actually display the image.

```
var image1 = new Image(480, 320);  //width, height
image1.src = "1.jpg"
```

Trimming blank spaces on strings

The newer browsers support the `trim` method to remove blanks on both ends of strings. This was not available before and you had to use a regular expression to trim strings. The new method is faster than using a `regex` as the following test demonstrates but you may need to add the `regex` method if you need to support older browsers. The `regex` that was compared was:

```
var y = x.replace(/^\s+|\s+$/gm,'');
```

⏱ PERFORMANCE TESTING	OPS (bigger is better)		
	Safari	Chrome	Firefox
1. Using str.trim()	8,076	11,058	18,351
2. Using regex	5,727	4,211	3,290

Test 3-17: http://www.nativeJavascript.com/tests/Test-TrimStrings.html

Dangers of premature optimization

It is usually good advice to avoid premature optimization. Get the general logic and program flow in place before you spend time optimizing certain areas or methods. You should concentrate on optimizing those areas of the program which are responsible for the majority of processing time. Use your debugging tools to determine which functions are taking up the most time and concentrate on optimizing those areas. That being said, I believe it is a good idea to always try to write for speed and smaller code. Once you learn the general concepts, you can write your code using those concepts.

Infinite scrolling on non-touch screens

Touch screens normally have to supporting scrolling using swiping movements. There are a number of libraries that add this functionality. I have used the *iScroll* library with great success. With just a couple lines of code, I can make any list or collection scrollable and it also allows me to independently scroll the list from the code. It supports touch events on touch-capable devices, or mouse events on PCs. If you need to add this kind of scrolling, or even infinite scrolling on discrete navigation interfaces, like a set-top box, or browsers using arrow buttons to scroll lists or a series of pictures, you can easily support this with minimal changes to the code.

The following is the general approach for a vertical scrolling list, such as a guide of TV shows. This assumes that the visible list contains 10 rows that you can scroll vertically by tapping an up or down arrow.

HTML

1. Create a clipping DIV element that is sized to display 10 rows and position it in the proper place. It should have a property of `overflow:hidden;`
2. As a child of that DIV, create another DIV that is sized to hold 12 rows. Set its `top` value to a negative amount equal to one row height. This results in row 0 and 11 being hidden, while rows 1-10 are shown.

JavaScript

1. Populate all 12 rows with data so that the top data row is in the second HTML row.

2. When the user presses a key, let's say the down button, use your animation routines to smoothly animate the large inner DIV that holds all 12 rows to end with an `top` value of a negative height equal to two rows.

3. Using a timer or an animation `transitionend` event, which fires after the DIV has moved, you need to have a function carry out several operations. First, it should fill in all 12 rows with new data, moving the data up one row. You can either copy the data from row to row, or fill in anew from your data source. Then, reposition your inner DIV back so its top value is a negative row height. These events will all happen at one time, so the user will not detect the movement.

You may want to optimize your routines using a `setTimeout` so that you don't immediately repopulate the grid if the user is pressing the up or down arrow very rapidly. With each key press, you can increment the index of the first data row to display, but wait until the user has not pressed a key for 200ms before you actually repopulate the data. Since the function that repopulates the grid is synchronous and may take some time, you want to defer that event as long as possible. You can also try moving the row elements around instead of just repopulating their data, but in general, I try to avoid messing around with the DOM in these cases.

"In theory, there is no difference between theory and practice. But, in practice, there is."

- Jan van de Snepscheut

4

Objects

JavaScript objects can be used to help organize and optimize your code. JavaScript's object model is based on prototypes as opposed to class inheritance. This means that you need to set up your objects differently than what you may be used to. It also means you need to understand how the prototype chain works when you create new objects or new instances of objects. There are a number of good books (like *The Principles of Object-Oriented JavaScript* by Nicholas C. Zakas or *Object-Oriented JavaScript* by Stoyan Stefanov) and web articles about how objects work in JavaScript so I will not go into that detail here. Instead I will cover some common uses of objects in your applications. I think you need to be very careful in using complicated objects and prototypes in your code as it can make your code slower and possibly harder to read. However, the proper use of objects will help minimize the amount of code you need and provide better protection of global name space.

Creating objects

There are several ways to create and use objects in your applications. You need to select the method that makes most sense for your needs. There is a difference in performance, so you want to select the simplest and clearest method.

1. **Plain object.** This uses the object constructor. This is the simplest but slower way to construct an object. All the properties are accessible on the object. You cannot use this to create unique instances of objects since any copy will reference the original object's values.

```
var newObj = {
  doThis: function() {},
  doThat: function() {},
  propOne:  12
};
```

2. **Regular object constructor.** This is the traditional object constructor. This is also very slow and is the slowest way by far to construct new object instances on Chrome. Values can be passed in to assign them to properties of the new object. All items declared with this are available on the object.

```
function ObjectConstructor(val) {
  this.type   = val || 0;
  this.doThis = function() {};
  this.doThat = function() {};
  this.propOne = 12;
}
var newObj = new ObjectConstructor(5);   //makes new instance
```

3. **Constructor with prototypes.** Similar to the previous constructor but uses `prototype` to add methods and properties which greatly speeds up the object creation. The prototype items are shared among instances created with this method. This is the fastest way by far to create object instances.

```
//OBJECT WITH PROTOTYPES
function ObjectsWithPrototypes() {}
ObjectsWithPrototypes.prototype.doThis = function() {};
ObjectsWithPrototypes.prototype.doThat = function() {};
ObjectsWithPrototypes.prototype.propOne = 12;
var newObj = new ObjectsWithPrototypes();  //makes new instance
```

4. **Module pattern.** This uses a closure and the `return` method to make whatever methods and variables you want exposed public. If items are not referenced in the return statement, they will be private to the object. Because the return statement returns a function, the main function can be used as a constructor. This method is in the middle of the list in terms of performance.

```
//MODULE PATTERN
var ModulePattern = (function() {
    function doThis() {}
    function doThat() {}
    var propOne = 12;
    return function() {
        this.doThis = doThis;
        this.doThat = doThat;
        this.propOne = propOne;
    };
  }());
var newObj = new ModulePattern();        //makes new instance
```

5. **Module pattern for singleton objects.** This is the same as the previous method except it is not a constructor. Only items referenced in the return statement are public. This is also very slow on Chrome.

```
//MODULE PATTERN FOR SINGLETON
var newObj = (function() {
    function doThis() {}
    function doThat() {}
    var propOne = 12;
    return  {
        doThis:  doThis,
        doThat:  doThat,
        propOne: propOne
    };
  }());
```

The following table gives some performance numbers for the times to construct new objects using the methods described above. It is a little hard to compare them since the constructors can actually be used to create multiple objects where the object in test 1 and 5 are just single objects.

PERFORMANCE TESTING	OPS (bigger is better)		
	Safari	Chrome	Firefox
1. Create - Plain object	218	16	15
2. Create - Regular constructor	212	1	16
3. Create - Constructor with prototypes	1,233	239	178
4. Create - Module pattern	67	31	69
5. Create - Module pattern - singleton	216	3	17

Test 4-1: http://www.nativeJavascript.com/tests/Test-CreatingObjects.html

Declaring methods for objects

When you are using a constructor for making object instances, there are several ways you can create methods for use by each instance:

- Include the method in your object constructor. The method will be duplicated and included in each instance. Changes to this method will not be reflected in any object instances already created.

- Add the method in a prototype statement. Each instance will share the same prototype method. Changes to the prototype method will affect all object instances. This is not normally used for handling properties you want to be unique for each object instance and it also won't have access to local variables in the constructor

- Add the method directly to an instance. Only this instance can access this method.

The following shows an object constructor with the effects of using the three different ways of assigning methods to objects.

```
//METHOD PART OF OBJECT
  function MakeObject() {
    this.doSomething = function() {
      console.log('Original method');
    }
  }
  var newInstance = new MakeObject();
  newInstance.doSomething();              //displays 'Original method'

//ADD PROTOTYPE BUT ORIGINAL METHOD STILL USED
  MakeObject.prototype.doSomething = function(){
    console.log('Prototype method');
  };
  newInstance.doSomething();              //displays 'Original method'

//DELETE METHOD ON INSTANCE - PROTOTYPE METHOD USED
  delete newInstance.doSomething;
  newInstance.doSomething();              //displays 'Prototype method'
```

```
//OVERRIDE PROTOTYPE METHOD - NEW PROTOTYPE METHOD USED
  MakeObject.prototype.doSomething = function(){
    console.log("New Prototype method");
  };
  newInstance.doSomething();             //displays 'New Prototype method'

//OVERRIDE METHOD ON INSTANCE - THIS METHOD USED
  newInstance.doSomething = function(){
    console.log("Override method");
  };
  newInstance.doSomething();             //displays 'Override method'

//DELETE INSTANCE METHOD - LAST PROTOTYPE METHOD USED
  delete newInstance.doSomething;
  newInstance.doSomething();             //displays 'New Prototype method'

//DELETE PROTOTYPE METHOD - METHOD NOW THROWS AN ERROR
  delete MakeObject.prototype.doSomething;
  // newInstance.doSomething();          //throws an error

//ASSIGN NEW PROTOTYPE METHOD - IT IS USED
  MakeObject.prototype.doSomething = function(){
    console.log("Last Prototype method");
  };
  newInstance.doSomething();             //displays 'Last Prototype method'
```

Deleting unused object references

When properties are de-referenced (go out of scope), they will be garbage collected. Thus, if you have a function that has local variables declared with `var,` when the function finishes, those variables will be garbage collected (gc'd). You don't need to do anything to them.

However, global objects and variables may persist even after you delete them. You need to be aware of how the different methods work depending on how the variables were declared in the first place.

- ♦ Variables can be set to `null`. This is actually a value. Depending on how the variable was declared, it may be garbage collected. However, global variables will have their memory freed but will not be completely removed by garbage collection.

- ♦ You can use the delete operator to complete remove most objects. However, a global object or variable that was declared using `var` (e.g. `var newVal = 4;`) is not removed and still contains its value.

- ♦ If you set a property of an object to `null`, then the null value is treated as a valid value and the property will not be gc'd. If you want to ensure these are cleared out, you can:

  a. Copy the object and its values to another object, omitting the value you want cleared. Then set the original object to `null`, or

  b. Use the delete command to delete the object property. However, this may have some impact on performance depending on the browser. You may just want to set the unused properties to null.

Newer browsers vary on how object methods and properties are stored and accessed. Some have been optimized to provide fast property lookup by using offsets instead of using a hash map. You don't want your lookups to be forced to use a hash map—you want the fast offset method. One thing you want to avoid is to change a "fast" lookup into a "slow" lookup. On some browsers, using the `delete` method will cause this to happen, resulting in more memory used and slower performance. Sparse arrays are slower for a similar reason. Instead, you should just set the property to `null` which will free up memory but will still leave the property set to null. Let's look at three consequences associated with removing object properties (this doesn't apply to the object itself—you can still remove the entire object.)

1. Speed in removing

I analyzed the relative performance of removing object properties using the delete method versus just setting the property (method or variable) to `null`. Obviously, if you just leave the property alone, there will be no performance hit, but you will be using memory that could be freed up. Setting to `null` also results in memory being used. The results were:

⏱ PERFORMANCE TESTING	OPS (bigger is better)		
	Safari	Chrome	Firefox
1. `delete obj.doThat;`	95	84	34
2. `obj.doThat = null;`	5,029	1,227	1,489

Test 4-2: http://www.nativeJavascript.com/tests/Test-ObjectsWithDelete.html

This measured how long it took to remove properties using the two methods. Setting the property to null still seems to have a significant edge in performance. I have noticed that the times of these methods has varied dramatically over browser versions so you should check before deciding which method to use.

2. Speed in accessing

Once the properties were removed, I tested the performance of accessing the remaining properties of the object. Test 3 measured the access speed of the object properties assuming I did not delete any properties to begin with.

⏱ PERFORMANCE TESTING	OPS (bigger is better)		
	Safari	Chrome	Firefox
1. `obj.doThat5();` //deleted other methods	73	1	45
2. `obj2.doThat5();` //set other methods to null	75	44	56
3. `obj3.doThat5();` //no methods removed	74	44	47

Test 4-3: http://www.nativeJavascript.com/tests/Test-AccessingDeletedProperties.html

This test showed very different results using recent browser versions. Using `delete` used to be much slower but the difference has almost disappeared except on Chrome where it is dramatically slower.

- The recommended method considering all these factors is to set your unused properties to `null` unless there is some reason that you have to use `delete`.

3. Memory usage

It is always hard to accurately measure memory of items that will be garbage collected but you still want to avoid creating garbage in the first place. However, the `delete` method can free up substantially more memory than setting object properties to `null`. Now that the performance of accessing objects with deleted properties seems to have improved, you may want to use delete to get rid of unused properties.

Assigning object properties

When assigning properties to singleton objects, you can save some code space and make your code easier to read by assigning them when the object is created. You should already be using the `{}` method of making objects, and not using `new Object()` as we discussed in an earlier chapter. And, instead of assigning properties like:

```
var newobj    = {};
newobj.prop1 = "a";
newobj.prop2 = "b";
```

use:

```
var newobj = {
      prop1:   "a",
      prop2:   "b"
   };
```

or use:

```
var newobj = {prop1:"a",prop2:"b"};
```

NOTE: If your object property names are not valid variable names, you can set their values using the `newobj["prop name"]` method or surround the name with quotes. Invalid names include those with embedded blanks or hyphens or those starting with a number. The speeds in the tests below were almost the same whether this method was used or the original method shown above was used.

PERFORMANCE TESTING	OPS (bigger is better)		
	Safari	Chrome	Firefox
1. Object first, then properties	65	4	1
2. Object and properties at same time	72	6	51
3. Array first, then elements	3	1	.4
4. Array and elements at same time	73	9	48

Test 4-4: http://www.nativeJavascript.com/tests/Test-AssigningObjectProperties.html

The above results test the speed of setting properties on objects using two methods, and also setting similar properties on arrays just for comparison. A few things this highlights:

◆ Firefox was very fast setting values on both objects and arrays if they were done at the same time the object was declared. Done separately, Firefox was really slow.

◆ Setting the values at the same time as the array was much faster on Chrome and Firefox.

♦ Results will vary with the browsers you need to support and the actual number of properties you need to set, but in terms of the speed of setting values, you most likely should set them, if possible, at the same time the object is declared. And, again if possible, arrays may be a better choice than objects in terms of speed of setting.

Getters and setters

The earlier methods of using `__defineGetter__()` and `__defineSetter__()` to define getters and setters have been deprecated. You should use `get` or `set` operators instead if you need this functionality. The general use of `get` and `set` is shown in the following object declaration:

```
var obj = {
  zip: 0,
  get zipcode(){
    return this.zip;
  },
  set zipcode(newval){
    this.zip= newval;
  },
  readzip: function() {
    return this.zip;
  }
};
  Object.defineProperty(obj, 'areacode', {
    value: 925
  });
obj.zipcode = 94563;       //use setter to set value of obj.zip
var newzip  = obj.zipcode;  //use getter to get value of obj.zip
var newzip2 = obj.readzip(); //use function to get value of obj.zip
```

The following tests show the differences in performance between using getters and setters, versus accessing the property directly versus using a regular object function to retrieve the value.

PERFORMANCE TESTING	OPS (bigger is better)		
	Safari	Chrome	Firefox
1. Setting object property using setter	25	.1	19
2. Setting object property directly	26	2	16
3. Reading object property using getter	24	.1	20
4. Reading object property directly	25	3	26
5. Reading object property using function	25	1	20

Test: 4-5: http://www.nativeJavascript.com/tests/Test-GettersAndSetters.html

What does this show us? There are a couple of conclusions. These are fairly new operators, and I have seen the browsers steadily improving, except for Chrome. For now, we can see:

♦ Except for Chrome, you pretty much can use whatever method is easiest. If you need to support Chrome, you should consider bypassing the use of the new getter and setter for now.

So why would you use these types of getters and setters?

1. You could use a setter to validate or even change the value passed in for the variable, or even change multiple object properties with the one value passed in. Of course, you could also do this with a regular method which might be faster.

2. You could simulate an overloaded method (which are not allowed in JavaScript) by adding a setter that allows the user to pass in a variable of different types (e.g. string, number, or object). Again you could also do this with a regular method that could also handle a varying number of arguments (the set operator can only accept one argument.)

3. You can use the `defineProperty` method of adding properties to objects to effectively create a read-only `Constant` value. Our previous definition of the `obj` object had the following code that added the new property `areacode` to our object. You can now access this property with the statement `obj.areacode` which will always return `925` and cannot be changed.

Using *this* and *that* with objects

You normally can use the special word `this` inside an object to refer to the properties of that object. However, there are a number of situations where the value of this will no longer refer to the object but to some other element. These situations include:

- **`setTimeout` and `setInterval` functions.** If your object contains code called in a timer, the value of `this` when the timer fires will be equal to the window.

- **Event handlers like click handlers.** Handlers set up in your object will have `this` referring to the event and not the object.

- **Callbacks.** Functions that use asynchronous callbacks such as AJAX calls will lose the reference to the object.

The usual way to avoid these problems is to assign another property of the object to be equivalent to the object's `this` property. The normal variable used is `that`, but some people use `self` instead. There is nothing special about this name. Whatever you use should be consistent across your installation to avoid confusion. The following example using an object constructor shows how this method can be used.

```javascript
var Cobj = function() {
  var that = this;
  this.a   = 4;
  this.b   = function() {
    console.log("a " + this.a);           // 4
  };
  this.d = function() {
    console.log("a " + this.a);           // 4
    setTimeout(function() {
      console.log("a2 " + this.a);        // undefined
      console.log("a3 " + that.a);        // 4
    },100);
  };
```

```
document.getElementById("idtest").onclick = function(e) {
    console.log("this a " + this.a);        // undefined
    console.log("that a " + that.a);        // 4
  };
};
var obj = new Cobj();
obj.b();
obj.d();
```

Enumerating properties of an object

There are several ways to enumerate the properties and property values of objects. Some may look easier but may have slow performance. These methods include:

1. `for (var name in obj)`. Use this to loop through all properties of the object. This will display all properties including inherited properties unless you check for `obj.hasOwnProperty(name)` for each name.

   ```
   for (var name in obj) {
    var val = obj[name];
   }
   ```

2. `Object.keys(obj)`. This returns an array of all enumerable property names. You can use this to get all the property values if needed.

   ```
   var arr  = Object.keys(obj);
   var alen = arr.length;
   for (var i=0; i < alen; i++) {
    var val = obj[arr[i]];
   }
   ```

3. `Object.getOwnPropertyNames(obj)`. This returns an array of all properties, enumerable or not, of an object.

   ```
   var arr  = Object.getOwnPropertyNames(obj);
   var alen = arr.length;
   for (var i=0; i < alen; i++) {
       var val = obj[arr[i]];
   }
   ```

PERFORMANCE TESTING	OPS (bigger is better)		
	Safari	Chrome	Firefox
1. for (var name in obj)	25	5	11
2. Object.keys(obj)	2	4	3
3. Object.getOwnPropertyNames(obj)	2	1	3

Test 4-6: http://www.nativeJavascript.com/tests/Test-EnumerateObjectProps.html

The fastest way on all the browsers was to use the standard `for (var name in obj)`. There may be other reasons to use one of the other methods but for simple enumerating this is fastest.

Comparing objects

If you compare objects to determine if they are the same, you need to be aware of the following conditions when you try to compare them:

- **Two objects made with the same constructor and values:** Not equal.
- **Two independent objects made with exactly the same properties:** Not equal.
- **A second object set equal to first object (e.g. obj2 = obj1):** Equal

5
HTML

Your application starts with your HTML file. Your HTML contains what your user will see and will determine how they will interact with your applications. We will discuss the CSS (Cascading Style Sheet) used to apply styles to your HTML elements in a later chapter. The other term you need to be familiar with is the *Document Object Model* or DOM. This model is the representation of all the elements that can be displayed by your application. It is often referred to as a "tree" since it is a hierarchical list of related elements.

Rule Number One

Don't mess with the DOM. Improper access and manipulation of the DOM tree is one of the major causes of poor application performance. You need to minimize the number of times the browser must reflow your document's DOM elements. An easy, and usually inadvertent, way of forcing a reflow is to simply ask to get an offset value, like `elem.offsetTop`. These methods force the browser to reflow the entire document in order to determine the exact value of the offset.

Rule Number Two

See rule number one.

How to add HTML elements to your application

There are several ways to add HTML elements to your application. You will have to decide which methods make sense for your application. Each method has its advantages and disadvantages. There are also a number of template systems and frameworks like Angular that are available that also handle adding HTML or dynamic HTML. The native methods include:

1. Place the elements in your main HTML file, usually called `index.html`. This may be useful if you have static HTML that isn't dynamically updated. In general, you want to have only the HTML loaded at the start that is needed for your initial screen display.

2. Append sections of HTML that you read in from files to the appropriate section of the existing HTML. This allows you to defer loading sections of the DOM until you need to.

3. Copy or clone existing elements and add them back into the DOM. You can change the values of any attribute before adding them to the DOM.

4. Create the elements from JavaScript using either `innerHTML` or `appendChild`. This allows you to create custom attributes and use loops to populate the DOM. An advantage of `appendChild` is that you can save the handle to the element at the time you create it if you need it later to change the element properties or content.

Getting to your first screen faster

You need to decide what to optimize for when designing your application. Sometimes you want to display the first screen as fast as possible; other times, you want to load more information first before displaying any interface or the full interface. Assuming you want to get your first screen displayed and operational as soon as possible, you need to keep the following in mind:

* Try to minimize the amount of JavaScript code that is needed to display the first screen. Instead, have most of the work done by your HTML and CSS.

* Have the initial file that is loaded (usually `index.html`) contain just the HTML that you need for your first page. Have your JavaScript load or create the rest after the first page loads.

* Put your `script` tags at the end of the document, after the HTML, to ensure that the HTML loads as fast as possible. Loading JavaScript files using `script` tags will block the complete display of your page. Most browsers will load script files in parallel but they still need to load.

* You normally do not want any JavaScript executing until your DOM is properly loaded. You can use one of two events (or both) on your body tag to call your initial function:
  * `onDOMContentLoaded`: This fires when the document is loaded and parsed, but images and stylesheets may not be loaded yet. If your HTML is complete in itself and doesn't need these items, this may work.
  * `onLoad`: This fires when the page is fully loaded. Since this waits for these other items, it may not fire for a while.

* Sometime it may be better to load more files and images when you start the app so that the application performs faster later. One part of UI design is deciding when and how to preload elements or information.

* You can also use the `defer` option in the `script` tag to defer loading of scripts that do not affect the DOM display. This is supported by most browsers now. Once the DOM has been loaded these files will then be requested and loaded.

See more information in Chapter 11 about loading JavaScript, HTML and CSS files.

Cloning nodes

If you have existing nodes you want to copy, you can use the `cloneNode` method to make copies. There are some advantages of creating elements this way, including:

* You can copy the node but then change individual properties before adding it back into the DOM. This can be useful for changing properties like ID or position.

* You can save the handle to the element if you need it later in your program.

An example of using this to copy an existing element is:

```
var rowelem   = document.getElementById('rowid-0');
for (var i=1; i < 10; i++) {
    var newNode   = rowelem.cloneNode(true);
    newNode.id    = 'rowid-' + i;
    parentobj.appendChild(newNode);
}
```

Ways to minimize your impact on the DOM

As discussed earlier, you want to minimize the times you have to force the browser to re-layout your HTML DOM. Sometimes this is unavoidable, but there are a number of methods you should use to keep this to a minimum.

1. Append an entire section of HTML read in from a file. This will cause a reflow but not multiple reflows for each element.

2. Use `innerHTML` to append a string containing many elements. This may also be faster than appending multiple elements.

3. Add new elements to a document fragment and then append that fragment to the DOM.

	PERFORMANCE TESTING	OPS (bigger is better)		
		Safari	Chrome	FireFox
1. `mdiv.innerHTML = str;`		41	31	21
2. `mdiv.appendChild(newDiv);`		63	18	21
3. `frag.appendChild(newDiv);`		64	26	30

Test 5-1: http://www.nativeJavascript.com/tests/Test-innerHTMLvsAppend.html

The results of testing using `innerHTML` vs `appendChild` showed different winners but they were all very close. Since your elements will most likely be more complicated than those used in the test, you probably need to test your exact requirements on each browser. Plus tests trying to measure performance when setting HTML elements in a loop are not very accurate in determine overall performance.

4. Don't access element attributes that require the browser to reflow the document. This includes items like: `offsetTop`, `offsetLeft`, etc. Instead, try to save these values to a variable or array when the elements are initially created or laid out, if possible, then use that value instead of querying the position. These operations can be very slow. The test below shows the difference between accessing the `offsetTop` property each time versus calculating it once and then accessing this saved value.

	PERFORMANCE TESTING	OPS (bigger is better)		
		Safari	Chrome	FireFox
1. `var divtop = divElem[i].offsetTop;`		381	162	406
2. `var divtop = divTop[i];`		98,457	55,480	83,718

Test 5-2: http://www.nativeJavascript.com/tests/Test-offsetTopvsCached.html

Using `offsetTop` or even `style.top` to access position attributes is much, much slower so avoid it as much as possible, particularly in loops.

5. Reuse - don't destroy and recreate. Try to lay out your displays so you share as many elements as possible, or at least reuse elements with only minimal changes. This may help reduce the reflow of elements, and reduces the amount of DOM manipulation.

6. Avoid changing attributes that will force reflow. This includes any positioning attribute like top or left, but does not include non-positioning attributes like color. Using absolute positioning can prevent reflow as well. A number of properties will also cause repaint

to occur which can also take time. I have also noticed cases where moving transparent images on top of backgrounds was slower than moving opaque images. This can also be a problem when displaying text on top of varying backgrounds since the character edges have to be anti-aliased against the background. Even a pseudo event like `hover` can cause a reflow so be careful with those.

Difference between visibility, opacity, and display

Once you have added elements to your DOM tree, there are several ways to temporarily hide them from the user. Each method has different advantages and disadvantages. You need to analyze each usage to make sure you have selected the proper method.

1. **Opacity**. You can set the element's `opacity` to zero (`opacity:0;`) to hide the element. This hides the element but does not change any of the layout. Plus, depending on how your elements are layered, the element may still intercept user mouse and touch events.

2. **Visibility**. You can set the element's `visibility` to `hidden` (`visibility:hidden;`) to hide the element. This hides the element but does not change the layout. However, it will no longer intercept user mouse and touch events.

3. **Display**. You can set the element's `display` property to none (`display:none;`) to hide the element. This removes the element from the DOM `display` tree. It is hidden, cannot accept user events, and does not affect the layout any more. Elements will be laid out by the display engine as if this element does not exist. If this is the desired effect, it should allow the rest of the UI to display faster since it doesn't have to lay out this element. You can also make changes to the element's attributes in this state without any penalty from having the layout refreshed.

Fading elements out: If you want to slowly fade an element, you can use a transition on the `opacity` attribute. If you want the user to be unable to touch or click on the hidden element, you will need to use a `timeout` set to the transition time to set the `visibility` to `hidden`, or the `display` property to `none`. after the opacity fade is done. Below is a sample of the CSS, HTML, and JavaScript function that show how this can be accomplished.

```
.fadeout {
  opacity: 1;
  -webkit-transition: opacity 200ms linear;
  -moz-transition: opacity 200ms linear;
  -o-transition: opacity 200ms linear;
  transition: opacity 200ms linear;
}
<div id="mvMain" class="fadeout"></div>
function fadeMain() {
  document.getElementById("mvMain").style.opacity = 0;
  setTimeout(function(){
    document.getElementById("mvMain").style.visibility="hidden";},200);
  }
}
```

Preventing elements from getting touch or click events. You may have an element that has either an opacity of zero or some low value to allow the element to act as a alpha layer on top of the rest of the UI. Since the element is visible, it will normally intercept all touch and click events. To keep this from happening, you can set the `pointer-events` CSS property to `none`:

```
pointer-events:none;
```

Dealing with inheritance. The `visibility` property is inherited, whereas `opacity` is not. You may run into problems if you have a parent container that holds a number of elements and you set the visibility property on the parent expecting the container and all its children to become invisible. However, if you have manually overridden the visibility property on one of the children, that will now take precedence and that element will no longer automatically inherit the visibility setting of its parent. Depending on your requirements, you may need to manually check the child elements or set/clear classes accordingly; use `display:none` on the children and let it inherit its `visibility` property, or set `visibility:inherit` when you make the child element visible.

Finding HTML elements

There are several ways in your JavaScript code to find elements in the DOM so you can act on them by changing their text, color, position, or other attributes. You should carefully design your HTML up front knowing which elements will need to be later accessed and changed. Some available methods make it easier to create more complicated search algorithms, but you usually pay for that convenience with slower performance.

The methods tested find elements based on their id, tag, or class. The `getElementsByName` should not be used any more as the `name` attribute has been deprecated. The three traditional methods are:

- `document.getElementById(id)`. Finds the first element with the designated id. Ids are supposed to be unique but that is not enforced and this method will only find the first one.

- `document[or element].getElementsByClassName(class)`. Returns an array of all elements that match the designated class name in the order the elements were found in the DOM. This array is a node list that is "live" meaning that any changes to the DOM will also change this list if it still exists. One advantage to this method is that it can be applied to any element in the DOM and not just the document. One major disadvantage is that it is inefficient if you keep the list and keep changing the DOM. Another disadvantage is that it is not supported on IE versions 8 and before. You can also use this method for two or more classes, such as `getElementByClassName`("class1 class2"). In this usage, the element must contain all the specified classes to be included in the array.

- `document.getElementsByTagName(tag)`. Returns an array of all elements with the designated tag (such as "div" or "p") in the order that they appear in the DOM. This array is a node list that is "live" meaning that any changes to the DOM will also change this list if it still exists. To get all elements in the DOM, use an asterisk (*) for the tag name.

A new method has been added that is supported by most browsers now. It allows you to do what the regular selectors do, in addition to using more selection criteria to make it easier to select elements. But that ease of use comes with performance penalties.

- `document[or element].querySelector(str)`. This returns the first element matching the designated string. Options for the argument include:
  - **ID**. Specify "`#id`".
  - **Class**. Specify ".`classname`".
  - **Tag**. Specify "`div`".
  - **Combination**. You can combine arguments, such as "`div.classname`".

- `document[or element].querySelectorAll(str)`. This returns an NodeList of all elements matching the designated string. The string options are the same as discussed above. This list is a "static" list which will not change, as opposed to the live list returned by `getElementsByClassName` and `getElementsByTagName`.

What method should you use? As stated before, it is most important to design your HTML with the proper IDs, tags, and classes based on what kind of access you will need from your Javascript code. The results below show performance trade-offs for using the different methods. A later chapter will briefly discuss the performance of using the jQuery $() selector.

🕐 PERFORMANCE TESTING	OPS (bigger is better)		
	Safari	Chrome	FireFox
1. `document.getElementById("div"+i);`	337	296	283
2. `document.getElementsByTagName("div");`	728	466	115
3. `document.getElementsByClassName("cname");`	809	513	122
4. `document.querySelector("#div"+i);`	188	203	35
5. `document.querySelectorAll("div");`	419	230	93
6. `document.querySelectorAll(".cname");`	466	262	81
7. `document.getElementById("onetime")`	29,454	19.005	999,999
8. `document.getElementsByClassName("onetime")`	13,760	8,163	5,748

Test 5-3: http://www.nativeJavascript.com/tests/Test-SelectingElement.html

The results are fairly consistent. However, there are a few lessons that you should keep in mind for your app. And don't forget that the results will vary depending on your exact application.

- The first method is slower than the others mainly because the element id has to be created by concatenating a string. Tests 7 and 8 test a simple fetch using a single string and shows that a regular `getElementById` is twice as fast as by class name, and on FireFox is hundreds times faster.

- The new `querySelector` and `querySelectorAll` are generally slower though it is hard to compare since they can do selections that you can't easily do in any other way. Thus, depending on how your HTML is structured, that might be a more efficient method. Or you may be able to restructure your DOM tree so that a more efficient single selector can be used.

The table below shows results of using a simple `getElementById` method and `querySelector` with a compound selector. `querySelector` is slower, but if you need it, use it.

PERFORMANCE TESTING	OPS (bigger is better)		
	Safari	Chrome	FireFox
1. `document.getElementById("div20a");`	381	288	12,336
2. `document.querySelector("div.newclass");`	24	8	14
3. `div20obj;    //cached reference`	13,408	9,102	12,192

Test 5-4: http://www.nativeJavascript.com/tests/Test-SimpleSelect.html

In general, you want to keep your DOM as flat as possible without excessive nested levels. Even excess comments in your HTML can slow down the browser. Some frameworks that dynamically create repeating HTML elements may replicate comments as well.

Binding events

In order to separate your display (views) from your code logic, it is usually better to avoid putting your event handler references directly in the HTML. Instead, add the handlers or listeners in your JavaScript code. Since some browsers (such as IE) don't set listeners the same way, you may need to add some utility functions such as the following:

```
//ALL EXCEPT IE<9
if (document.getElementById("BODY").addEventListener) {
    var addEvent = function(elem,event,cback,opt) {
        opt = opt || false;
        try {elem.addEventListener(event,cback,opt);}
        catch(e){};
    };
    var removeEvent = function(elem,event,cback,opt) {
        opt = opt || false;
        try {elem.removeEventListener(event,cback,opt);}
        catch(e){};
    };
//IE<9 - bubble phase only
} else {
    var addEvent = function(elem,event,cback) {
        elem.attachEvent(event,cback);
    };
    var removeEvent = function(elem,event,cback) {
        elem.detachEvent(event,cback);
    };
};
```

It is better to do these tests and set the methods once when your app starts instead of checking every time you have to add or remove a listener. Using the above code, to set a listener on element "elem" for a "mouseup" event, you would use code such as:

```
addEvent(elem,"mouseup",callbackFunction,false);
```

The last argument (`false` = default) indicates that events will bubble up the DOM tree from the element to the top of the tree. Specify `true` to execute the handler during the capture phase. This is useful for immediately capturing events and stopping their propagation using `stopPropagation` or `cancelBubble`. This is discussed in more detail in the Event Handling chapter.

Using ID's to identify elements

Each ID in your DOM should be unique. Though not absolutely enforced, any attempt to use `getElementById` finds the first element with that ID. Tag, class, and name fields can be duplicated as needed. An easy way to set unique ID's accessible from loops is to append a number to the end of a string. You can't start ID's with numbers, but you can end them with numbers. The plus sign, hyphen, and underscore are valid characters in ID names. Names might look like:

```
<div id="name_full-0">John Doe</div>
<div id="name_full-1">Jane Doe</div>
```

That way, you can access these elements in a loop, such as:

```
for (var i=0; i < 2; i++) {
    document.getElementById("name_full-"+i).innerHTML = names[i];
}
```

You can also use other methods to locate your elements by their class or ID. Your exact application will dictate the best method.

innerText vs. innerHTML

There are several ways to add text or HTML to existing DOM elements. Depending on what you are trying to add, you need to be sure you select the correct method. Two methods handle just text while innerHTML will let you add HTML tags and text. Some methods didn't work with older browsers but should work with most current browsers. These methods can be used to either set or get the content. There are other differences between the methods:

- `innerHTML`: This lets you add HTML tags but is slower than innerText because of the extra layout. Be careful using it because it will replace all the HTML content inside the element. If you need to add HTML tags, then this is the method you must use.

- `innerText`: Sets or gets just the text of the element and not any HTML tags. It will not return the text of elements that are hidden. If you are adding simple text to your element and don't need to add HTML tags, this method is more than 10 times faster than the other two methods. It does not force a reflow of your DOM so it executes much faster.

- `textContent`: Similar to `innerText` but will get content of all elements including script and style tags, and also return content that is hidden.

- `nodeValue`: You can examine the `nodeValue` property of the `firstChild` property of the element if your text is located in that position.

PERFORMANCE TESTING	OPS (bigger is better)		
	Safari	Chrome	FireFox
1. `elem.innerHTML = "text";`	513	136	482
2. `elem.innerText = "text";`	9,873	2,468	370
3. `elem.textContent = "text";`	2,880	13,943	674
4. `elem.firstChild.nodeValue = "text";`	18,558	11,422	1,024
5. `var txt = elem.innerHTML;`	4,946	2,925	999,999
6. `var txt = elem.innerText;`	563	821	2,210
7. `var txt = elem.textContent;`	16,591	10,506	7,849
8. `var txt = elem.firstChild.nodeValue;`	21,055	13,173	999,999

Test 5-5: http://www.nativeJavascript.com/tests/Test-innerHTML.html

If you are setting text, using `nodeValue` has fairly good performance but if you need to set HTML properties, you must use `innerHTML`. Likewise, reading elements was faster using `nodeValue` if you can use it with your elements. Firefox has greatly optimized reading text with `innerHTML` so that is an option. Plus some of the other methods act slightly differently with different browsers when returning some text like line breaks so you need to test your application. The following simple code has different results when you examine it with the different measures. You may get the CR/LF characters in your response when you were not expecting it.

HTML CODE

```
<div id="div1">
  <span id="span1" style="left: 10px;">Inside Span</span>
  <span style="display:none;">Inside display none span</span>
</div>
```

- **Output using innerHTML of div1**

```
<blank line here>
<span id="span1" style="left: 10px;">Inside Span</span>
<span style="display:none;">Inside display none span</span>
<blank line here>
```

- **Output using innerText of div1**

```
Inside Span
```

- **Output using textContent of div1**

```
<blank line here>
Inside Span
Inside display none span
<blank line here>
```

Appending text in the DOM

We have discussed using `innerHTML`, `innerText`, and `textContent` to add new content to your DOM. There is another method, `insertAdjacentHTML`, that can also insert content into existing elements. There are four positions that can be specified--`beforebegin`, `afterbegin`, `beforeend`, and `afterend`. You specify the new information as a text string. It can be helpful in appending new information to existing display, such as a news feed or list of blog comments. However, it is not as fast as other methods in most cases but you should test your specific use. The code snippet used in the following test looked like:

```
var elem = document.getElementById("test3");
elem.insertAdjacentHTML('beforeend', ('<span>abc' + i + '</span>'));
```

⏱ PERFORMANCE TESTING	OPS (bigger is better)		
	Safari	Chrome	FireFox
1. Build string then innerHTML = str	31	14	30
2. Use innerHTML += str	4	3	4
3. Use insertAdjacentHTML	15	5	13
4. Use appendChild	82	17	25

Test 5-6: http://www.nativeJavascript.com/tests/Test-insertAdjacent.html

Getting images to display faster

Improper use of images can make your app slower to load and display, and can affect the speed of UI navigation. There are a number of things you can do when designing your application, including:

- Minimize the number of images you use in your application.

- Use solid background colors instead of images.

- Design your screens so that you share as many UI elements as possible. Besides minimizing the number of elements that have to be loaded, your screen transitions should be smoother without any flashes.

- Combine your smaller images into bigger images so you can load them as sprites, discussed below.

- If you have to use an image, make sure it is created at the exact size that the UI uses to display. Don't request a larger image that takes up bandwidth only to have the browser scale the image to a smaller size. Plus, you can usually use your graphics editing tool to create a better looking smaller image.

- Include size attributes with your image tags to enable the browser to properly size and position the image even before it has been fetched and rendered. Failure to do this results in web pages that hop around as images finally load. For tables, you can specify `table-layout: fixed;` to avoid table columns and rows from resizing.

- Use special font characters for simple icons and other one-color images. Using font characters has several benefits:

  - The one font file will load much faster than a number of separate image files.

  - The font characters can be scaled to any size and still look smooth since they are essentially vector images. They can be really big or really small.

  - The font characters will normally be anti-aliased (edges smoothed using color variations) against whatever color background they are displayed over. This eliminates the need to have the same transparent `gif` or `png` image duplicated against different backgrounds so that they are properly anti-aliased.

  - Special font characters will display faster in tables once the font has loaded rather than waiting for images to load and be rendered.

  - It is easy to change the color of a font character image to indicate a special state.

  - Checkboxes. You may find it easier to use a font checkbox character if you need a checkbox in a table column. You can use a click handler to alternate the character between an empty box character and a box that contains a checkmark. This may be faster and smaller than putting an input checkbox control on every line.

  - You can find a number of common symbols on websites like `https://icomoon.io/` or use a good font-editor to make almost any one-color image you want: 🏠 🎨 ✉ ◀ ▶ ★ ↻ ♪ ⬆ ⬇ ⬆ ⬇ ● 🔒 ♥

- There are several methods to use to display your special font characters.
  1. Set up a class that is used every time you want to display a special character, then include that character inside a <span> or <div> element.

```
.specialFont {
  font-family: iconfont;
  font-size: 15px;
  color: #ee3333;
}
<div class="specialFont">C</div>
```

  2. Set up a class that uses the `before` selector:

```
.specialChar:before {
  font-family: iconfont;
  content: "\e653";
  color: #993333;
}
<span class="specialChar"></span>
```

There are a few methods you can use in your code to improve the performance of your images.

1. **Preload your images**. Preloading references images before you actually need them, forcing the browser to fetch them into local cache before you show them. This increases the speed at which display. The easiest way is to build an image array in your JavaScript and load images into that array. Future requests for those images will be faster because the image will already be cached. Normally, you will also want to put this code in a function that is not called until the first page is loaded so that you can display that first page faster.

```
imageNames    = ["pic1.png","pic2.png","pic3.png"];
var imgNum     = imageNames.length;
var imageList = [];
for (var i=0; i < imgNum; i++) {
    imageList[i]     = new Image();
    imageList[i].src = imageNames[i];
}
```

2. **Sprites**. Sprites are smaller images combined into one larger image. The single image loads faster than multiple smaller images due to the overhead of fetching files. Your CSS defines which sections of the large image to display in different places in your UI. This method is often used to combine the normal/hover/selected/disabled versions of icons. The following example assumes you have combined several images, each 60px by 60px, into one large `picbig.png`. The numbers in the background statement represent the position of the image—horizontal first and then vertical. They are negative numbers as they represent where the top left of the image will be positioned resulting in the desired part of the image showing through the 'window' created by the `height` and `width` values.

```
.imageOne {
    height:60px;
    width:60px;
    background:url('picbig.png') 0 0;
}
.imageTwo {
    height: 60px;
    width: 60px;
    background:url('picbig.png') -60px 0;
}
```

3. **On/off images on top of each other.** You often have images that change appearance when touched or clicked on, such as an icon that shows state, or even a manually created radio button. One method of changing state is to just replace the first image with the second image. You may get better performance by putting both versions of the image on top of each other and then just hiding or showing the topmost image to show the change in state.

4. **Forcing image decompression.** The first part of getting faster image performance was getting the original image cached locally. The second part is to speed up the decompression and actual display of the image. If you have a display that handles a lot of images that the user can scroll through, you may want to speed up the image display as much as possible. Images that are off-screen or hidden may take longer to display when you want them on screen. One option is to add to each image a border of a few pixels that is transparent (if the image is a `png` or `gif`), or colored to match the background. Then, display the images that will be displayed next positioned to be actually only 1 or 2 pixels on the screen. This will force the browser to decompress and actually display the image before the user swipes it onto the screen.

6

CSS Techniques

You can use Cascading Style Sheets (CSS) to format your HTML displays. With the release of CSS 3, your applications can now take advantage of many powerful new features that add animation, drop shadows, and more display control for mobile devices. This chapter is not a CSS reference manual or a detailed description of each CSS property but rather a collection of some general comments about common CSS uses and problems.

Including CSS in your application

There are several ways to add CSS styling to your HTML apps. You should be aware of the strengths and weaknesses of each method and decide accordingly. Your optimum solution may even be a combination of two or more of the methods. The methods include:

1. Adding your CSS definitions inside <style></style> tags in your HTML. These would have to be repeated inside each HTML file the definitions are used for.

2. Put your CSS definitions in a separate CSS file that you include inside your HTML by specifying something similar to the following inside your head tag. This allows one CSS definition file to be used by multiple HTML files and load faster since it will be cached locally after the first access, but you will have to include a reference to this file in each of your HTML files.

   ```
   <link rel="stylesheet" href="index.css" type="text/css">
   ```

3. Load an external CSS file from inside your JavaScript code using an XMLHttpRequest method. This may be useful if you want to delay loading some files, or if the CSS is only needed some of the time, or if you need to load different CSS files based on some value available at runtime. You may have subdirectories of CSS organized by theme or company name and you may want to select which ones to load.

4. Include the necessary CSS properties directly inline in the HTML tags. This is generally not recommended as it doesn't allow the display to be separated from the data and styles cannot be shared but are actually overridden.

5. Use JavaScript commands to assign style attributes or classes to specific elements.

Position property

In laying out your screens, you need to decide if you are going to use absolute positioning or rely on letting the normal flow determine the position of the elements. In designing mobile phone applications, I usually rely on absolute positioning to ensure text and graphics line up properly. Websites or apps that contain more random data may do better to use static or relative positioning. One advantage of absolute positioning is that the entire document does not have to reflow if you move one element.

- **static**: (default). The element is positioned in the position determined by the normal flow of the page.
- **relative**: You can set left or top values to move the element relative to its normal flow position. But the original position and size is saved and used for positioning the next static or relative element.
- **absolute**: Specifying a top and left value positions the element at this position relative to its container. It does not affect how other static or relative elements are positioned.
- **fixed**: Specifying a top and left value fixes the element's position in the window and not the parent container. This is useful for fixed menus and lists that you don't want to move when the user scrolls the screen.
- **inherit**: Inherits the position property of the element's parent.

Display property

Use the display property to select the type of "box" the element is displayed in. It also has an important use when set to "none" in removing the element from the display layout.

- **inline:** (default) Displays the element inline inside the current block using the width of the content, similar to a <span> tag.
- **block**: Displays the element as a block with a specified height and width, like a <p> tag.
- **inline-block**: Displays the element inline but treats as a block.
- **none**: This removes the element from the DOM display tree. This can be used to update the removed element without forcing a reflow, or to temporarily remove elements to "lighten up" the DOM for better performance.
- **Others**: There are a number of other options which may not work on older browsers, such as: table, table-cell, run-in, list-item, inline-table. See your CSS documentation for more details. Since the use of the <table> tag on anything other than a table of data is discouraged, the use of some of the table display properties (like `table-cell`) can solve some of your UI problems like vertical alignment.

Setting style properties using JavaScript

There are several ways to change the style of elements from JavaScript. They each have their uses, advantages, and disadvantages. It is more important to design your UI pages properly to minimize the amount of style manipulation needed. The most common reason to set individual properties (either directly or using `cssText`) is when you need to do this dynamically from your JavaScript code to set a new position or color property. These methods include:

- **Assigning a new class or classes using `className`.** This is usually the fastest method to change styles and style properties. Any individual style properties that have already been assigned (using `cssText` or `style=`) will not be overridden but still have precedence.

- **Assigning a new class using classList.** The classList property has `add` and `remove` methods that can be used to change classes.

- **Append a new class to the existing className.** This uses the '+=' operator to append a new class to the element. Be sure to include a blank before each class name.

- **Assigning individual style attributes.** This is most useful when you have a variable property value you must assign from JavaScript, such as a position or color. Depending on how many attributes you must assign, it is usually faster than using cssText.

- **Assigning multiple styles attributes using cssText.** cssText allows you to read or set multiple style attributes in one command. You would think it would be faster than assigning the properties individually, but is usually slower except on Firefox. It does clear out any previous properties assigned using `style`.

Setup for performance tests below:

```
.classOne {
    left: 10px;
    color: #ff9900;
}
.classTwo {
    top: 10px;
    height: 10px;
}
function addClass(elem, className) {
    elem.className += " " + className;
}
```

⏲ PERFORMANCE TESTING	OPS (bigger is better)		
	Safari	Chrome	FireFox
1. element.className = "classOne classTwo";	11,755	2,610	5,306
2. element.classList.add("classOne"); element.classList.add("classTwo");	749	404	75
3. addClass(element, "classOne"); addClass(element, "classTwo");	883	461	81
4. element.className += " classOne"; element.className += " classTwo";	809	494	97
5. element.style.left = "10px"; element.style.color = "#ff9900"; element.style.top = "10px"; element.style.height = "10px";	1,305	582	109
6. element.style.cssText = "left:10px; color:#ff9900; top:10px; height:10px;";	264	436	152
7. element.className = "classOne"; element.className += "classTwo";	1,305	848	94

Test 6-1: http://www.nativeJavascript.com/tests/Test-CssSetClass.html

The fastest method of assigning new style properties will be using `className` and assigning multiple classes at the same time if needed. If you need to override individual properties, setting them individually is faster than using `cssText` except on FireFox.

NOTE: When you use `cssText` to set style properties, it will remove all other properties that were previously assigned using `element.style` but will not remove properties assigned by a `class` (though it will override them.)

CSS selectors

Many CSS properties are inherited from their parent elements but not all properties are. You need to refer to a CSS reference if you are unsure about a specific property's inheritance.

The order that CSS rules are applied to your elements in determined by their specificity. You need to be careful when you design your HTML that you either avoid specificity problems or incorporate them properly into your design. Browsers weigh the CSS selectors that might apply to each element in your HTML. When multiple selectors have equal specificities, the latest declarations apply. Rules that are applied directly to an element take precedence over inherited rules. The following list shows the general precedence order, from least to most specific.

1. Universal * selector
2. Pseudo elements and type selectors
3. Class selectors and pseudo classes
4. ID selectors
5. Inline styles on element *(this one wins!)*

Overwriting style using the !important rule

Styles declared with the addition of `!important` on the declaration will override other declarations that may apply to that element. Two rules that both have `!important` will use the specificity rules described above. Generally, you should avoid use of `!important` and instead structure your CSS so that it is not required, though this may not always be possible.

There are many articles, books, and websites devoted to explaining the rules of CSS precedence. If the rules are that complicated (and they are), my suggested approach would be to avoid relying on subtle interactions of CSS rules and instead focus on making simple CSS rules that are as specific as possible as often as possible. This avoids interactions that may be difficult to trace and debug, and made actually improve performance. If in doubt, simplify.

Descendant selectors

Descendant selectors are multiple selectors defined together, such as:

```
.class1 .class2 { props... }
```

You can chain all types of selectors together—including element, class, and type. It is a feature of CSS and can be leveraged to make your CSS easier to assign. Some CSS compilers (like LESS) also produce this kind of CSS output by allowing you to nest CSS definitions. However, I recommend against overuse of this style for several reasons:

1. It can make your HTML harder to read since you have to examine the ancestors of elements to determine which selector actually applies.

2. Depending on how they are written, they can be less efficient than more directed selectors.

3. If you need to change the appearance of an element that uses one of these nested classes, it will be very difficult both to determine what to do and to avoid changing other elements.

The inefficiency of descendant selectors usually arises when programmers are not aware of how they are assigned. The selectors are actually examined from right to left to determine which element or elements they apply to. Consider the following CSS selector:

```
div#elemid li.liclass
```

The browser must perform the following calculations to resolve this selector. And I have seen many selectors that are much more complicated.

1. Find all elements with `class = liclass`

2. Select only elements from this list that are `li` elements

3. Narrow this list down to only elements with `ID = elemid`

4. Now collect only those elements that are `divs`

I have seen descendant selectors as bad or worse than the following and this was not generated by a CSS compiler (tell me how easy this would be to change or debug). Note: A number of the following declarations are separated by commas which does not make them descendant selectors but rather lets you assign the same properties to all the selectors separated by commas.

```
#ng-container .vid-header .container .vid-favorites-container .vid-top-
right-nav .vid-saved-searches-list .vid-saved-searches-ul li .vid-fav-
doc-dir-pane a.vid-saved-search-menu-url:hover,
#ng-container .vid-header .container .vid-favorites-container .vid-top-
right-nav .vid-saved-searches-list .vid-fav-docs-ul li .vid-saved-search-
pane a.vid-saved-search-menu-url:hover,
favorites-container .vid-top-right-nav .vid-saved-searches-list .vid-
saved-searches-ul li a.vid-saved-search-menu-url:hover,
#ng-container .vid-header .container .vid-favorites-container .vid-top-
right-nav .vid-pop-searches-list .vid-saved-searches-ul li .vid-saved-
search-pane a.vid-saved-search-menu-url:hover {
   color: #1ba5e1;
}
```

But there are times when using descendant selectors makes a lot of sense. You may have a large number of elements grouped under a parent that may all change appearance when the parent class is changed. For example, you might want the Title and Description to change color when the parent theme changes in the following example:

```
<div id="eParent" class="theme-one">
  <div class="child-one">Title</div>
  <div class="child-two">Description</div>
</div>
```

So you could have CSS that looks like:

```
.theme-one {
  //properties for theme one
}
.theme-two {
  //properties for theme two
}
.theme-one .child-one {
  color: red;
}
.theme-one .child-two {
  color: red;
}
.theme-two .child-one {
  color: blue;
}
.theme-two .child-two {
  color: blue;
}
```

Changing the class on the parent (`id=eParent`) from `theme-one` to `theme-two` changes the color of its children from red to blue. The use of descendant selectors can be powerful.

Remove unused CSS declarations

Another often overlooked target for optimization is unused CSS declarations. It is way too easy to bloat your CSS files using cut and paste or not removing unused selectors as you change your HTML. Removing those unused declarations will speed up rendering as well as conserve bandwidth by making your files smaller. There are a number of tools out there that will help in removing unused CSS. You can open up the Audits tab in the Chrome Developer Tools and run an audit to display an option to `Remove unused CSS selectors`. Be careful as the tool checks for CSS on the current page only and it may not find classes that might be dynamically created. You may have to use global searches as well.

Be careful with expensive CSS properties

There are a number of CSS properties that are more expensive than others due to the extra strain they place on browsers trying to lay out and repaint your web page. You probably know which properties might be expensive by just envisioning the extra work the browser must do to render the element properly. These properties include:

- shadows
- transforms and transitions
- transparency of any type since items are anti-aliased on layers below
- opacity
- gradients
- border-radius (this one is easy to overuse but was one of the more expensive properties

So try your best to remove as many of these as possible without compromising the look of your UI. If you are rotating text that doesn't change, consider making it an image. Gradients can be replaced with solid colors

CSS box model

A key to understanding how your elements are positioned is knowing the relationship of the various element size and padding values. The CSS *box model* refers to the way browsers position and space content based on the following properties of each element:

* padding
* border
* margin

When you specify the height and width of an element, you are specifying the size of the inside element. The total size of the element is then calculated by adding in the values for padding, border and margin to get the total size of the element. Thus, the 100 pixel wide element you think should fit may actually be taking up a lot more space when you add in the padding, border, and margin values.

To allow for these additions when designing your UI, you can normally handle the situation in one of two ways:

* Make the width and height properties smaller to allow for the added padding, margin, and border space. You would have to calculate how much smaller to make the inner element to fit your design, or
* Use the CSS property: `boxSizing` to make your design easier. The default value is `content-box` which is essentially described above. You can specify the following to make your width and height properties include your padding and border values (but not margin): **box-sizing: border-box;**

We can easily visualize this using the box model that most browsers display in their debug console when you are inspecting any HTML element. We can set up a div element using the following class definition perhaps expecting a element 100 pixels wide.

```
.test {
  top: 10px;
  left: 20px;
  width: 100px;
  height: 70px;
  padding: 2px 4px 2px 4px;
  border: 3px solid black;
  margin: 5px;
}
```

However, the final width may not be what you were expecting. Most of the browser debuggers will display the exact values for the margin, border, and padding in a visual box display. When you look at the actual box model in the debugger, you will see something like the following:

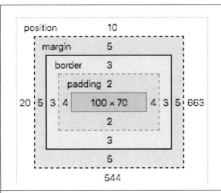	**content-box (default)** The total width is now the `width` plus `padding` plus `border` plus `margin`. For our example, this equals (100 + 8 + 6 + 10) or 124 pixels. If this element is not positioned absolutely, the following elements will start 124 pixels over. The same adjustments happen to the height.

If we now add the following property to the class, `box-sizing: border-box;` we will see the following.

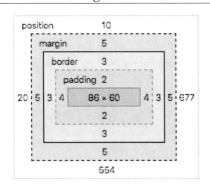	**border-box** You see now that the element width has essentially been reduced so that the `width` plus `padding` plus `border` equal the original specified width. This means the element's `width` is essentially reduced to 86 pixels. The margin will still be added to this resulting in a total width of 110 pixels. But you often will not have a margin which means the result of 100 pixels will match your expected width. The same adjustments happen to the height.

Making text selectable

Most of the time, you do not want the elements of your pages to be selectable by the user. If you have elements in text boxes, they will normally be selectable but other text in div and span elements may not be. You may want to set up two CSS classes that you can use to assign to the elements you want the user to be able to select, usually to copy it to another program.

```
.unselectable {
    user-select:         none;
    -moz-user-select:    none;
    -khtml-user-select:  none;
    -webkit-user-select: none;
    -o-user-select:      none;
}

.selectable {
    user-select:         all;
    -moz-user-select:    all;
    -khtml-user-select:  all;
    -webkit-user-select: all;
    -o-user-select:      all;
}
```

Centering elements

This is a favorite interview question that I have heard in multiple interviews. It is also something that you will probably be doing all the time. Horizontally centering text inside an element is simple using the `text-align:center;` property. However, centering elements like div elements inside other elements is a little harder.

Centering text

- **Horizontally.** This is usually done with assigning a style to the containing element similar to the following (or by using a CSS class). This will horizontally center the text inside the `div` element no matter how many lines it appears on.

  ```
  <div style="text-align: center;">Centered Text</div>
  ```

- **Vertically—one line of text.** There are two quick ways to do this if you know the size of the container and are sure there will be only one line of text. Otherwise, you should use the method below that will vertically center multiple lines of text. The ways are:

  - **Using line height.** Set the `line-height` property to the height of the container that holds the text, similar to:

    ```
    <div style="height: 64px; line-height: 64px;">This is text</div>
    ```

  - **Using padding.** Set the `padding-top` property to a value that will vertically center the text. You may have to experiment some with this value to get it correct.

    ```
    <div style="height: 64px; padding-top: 24px;">This is text</div>
    ```

- **Vertically—multiple lines of text.** This works with one line or multiple lines and uses a feature of the `display` property. The use of tables for positioning is frowned upon, but there are a number of table properties that you can assign to any element using the `display` property. By assigning a value of `table-cell` to the container, you can then use the `vertical-align` property to center your text, similar to:

  ```
  <div style="height:100px;display:table-cell;vertical-align:middle;">
     This is text
  </div>
  ```

Centering div elements (or elements with display: block property)

Centering div or block type elements is a little more complicated but there is a relatively simple way to center them in both directions. The element to center has to have a fixed width and height for this method to work. If these values may change, then you will have to use a property of auto and then have JavaScript code check for the height and width after the element displays. This method relies on using relative positioning of 50% and then negative margins to center the item. The margin values have to be set to a negative value of one-half the width or height. To center an element in both directions, you can use code similar to:

```
<div style="width:200px; height:200px;">
   <div style="position:relative; width:80px; height:20px; top:50%;
       left:50%; margin-left:-40px; margin-top:-10px;"></div>
</div>
```

Other CSS properties I often forget

In addition to the `box-sizing` property described above, I always seem to forget the following properties:

- `pointer-events: none;` You can apply this to transparent or semi-transparent objects that are overlaying other objects on your screen to allow mouse events to pass through to the lower element and not be intercepted by this element.

- `table-layout: fixed;` Instead of making column widths based on the content in each cell, the table size is fixed to the values you specify for the table and each column. This forces tables to look consistent and will also speed up display since the browser can display the table right away without waiting to place all the content.

- `white-space: nowrap;` This prevents long strings from wrapping onto subsequent lines and forces it to one line.

7
Event Handling

JavaScript has a number of ways to assign and handle mouse, keyboard, and touch events. It can be confusing to know exactly which method to use to assign handlers, and how to properly handle them to avoid breaking your application. I think there is also some uncertainty about how events are actually handled inside your document. There are all types of events that you will be handling in your code, including document load events and key handling events, but I will concentrate on input events that I think cause the most problems.

There are several concepts that need to be understood concerning setting and using event handlers. These include:

- Setting handlers
- Understanding the order events are handled, including the concept of capture vs. bubble stages
- Controlling the propagation of events through multiple handlers

Setting event handlers

You can use a variety of methods to assign event handlers to elements. These methods are all different and are covered in more detail below. These methods include:

1. `element.attachEvent()`: IE8 and earlier only
2. HTML assignment: such as `<div onclick="doSomething()">`
3. direct assignment from JavaScript: such as `element.onclick=doSomething;`
4. `element.addEventListener`: all browsers; IE9 and later. This is the recommended method as it separates code from HTML as well as having more flexibility.

Order of event handling

There are three orders of event handling you need to be concerned with:

1. Multiple handlers for the same event on the same element.
2. Multiple handlers for different events on the same element.
3. Multiple handlers for the same event on different elements.

You can even assign several handlers for the same event to the same element. You need to be aware of how your browser handles those multiple handlers.

- **Multiple handlers for same event on same element**. You can assign two or more handlers for the same event to an element, like two `onClick` handlers. They should fire in the order they were assigned but I would not rely on this. Because of the possible ambiguity of doing this, I strongly recommend against doing this. You are only asking for problems.

- **Multiple handlers for different events on same element**. There is a standard order that events will fire when you click on an element or press a key. You need to be aware of this when you assign your handlers. The order for standard mouse events is:
    1. mousedown
    2. mouseup
    3. click
    4. submit (if this applies)

    The order for key events is:
    1. keydown
    2. keypress
    3. keyup

- **Multiple handlers for the same event on different elements**. Each document normally consists of a series of nested elements, starting with the BODY tag and moving down through your DOM. You may have a DIV that contains other DIV elements, SPAN elements, or even FORM elements. When you create an event on an element (like clicking on it), the browser walks the DOM in two directions, passing the event to any handlers that have been assigned. First, in the *capture* phase, the event will move from the top, outermost element down to the element that was acted upon. Once it reaches that element, it then *bubbles* back up to the outermost, top element. Any handler for this event on any of those elements will be executed.

    However, it is more complicated than that. All regular handlers work only on the *bubble* stage. Thus, they don't get any of the events that were created during the *capture* stage. There is only one way to see the *capture* events, and that is assigning handlers using the `addEventListener` method, specifying the correct argument. This method works on all browsers except IE8 and earlier.

Event propagation

Events are automatically passed to parent and children elements following the *capture* and *bubble* stages discussed above. If you do not want this default behavior, you must add methods to your event handlers to stop this propagation. You will see several methods called from within event handlers to stop or alter how events are either handled or propagated. It is important to understand the differences between these methods as it is easy to use the wrong method.

- `event.stopPropagation()`. This stops the propagation of the current event but has no effect on other events that may have handlers. This works in both capture and bubble stages. If you call `stopPropagation` in an event handler registered as a capture handler on an element at the top of your DOM tree, that event will never reach any other handler.

- `event.cancelBubble = true`. This acts similar to `stopPropagation` but is only used for IE 8 and earlier versions. If you need to support those browsers, you will need to handle both methods.

- `preventDefault()`: This is used ONLY to cancel the default action of the event. You may want to have an event handler on a submit button that checks for error conditions and ensures all fields are filled in before actually submitting a form. Not all events are cancelable but you can check the event's `cancelable` property to determine its eligibility. The `preventDefault` method DOES NOT stop the event from propagating. You still need to use one of the above methods for that. It is mainly used to stop the following two types of actions:
    - clicking on a form `submit` button to submit the form
    - clicking on an `<a href>` tag to open a link

- `return false`: This one is very interesting and is probably the most misunderstood method and for good reasons because *it depends...*
    - `addEventListener`: For handlers set with this method, `return false` has NO EFFECT. You must use `stopPropagation` and/or `preventDefault` as needed.

    - HTML assignment: If you assign the handler directly on the element, like the following code, then a `return false` in the handler will stop the default action but NOT stop propagation. You have to include the `return` in the onclick string.

      ```
      <div onclick    = "return doSomething();"> or
      element.onclick = doSomething;
      ```
    - `attachEvent`: For handlers set with this method (IE 8 or before), `return false` will prevent the default action but NOT stop propagation.
    - jQuery handlers: For handlers set up using jQuery, `return false` will both stop propagation and prevent the default action. This is probably the source of most of the confusion.

Using *addEventListener*

You can add handlers to your elements from JavaScript using the `addEventListener` method:

```
element1.addEventListener('click', doClick, true);   or

element1.addEventListener('click', doClick, false);
```

Both of these methods add a click handler to `element1` that will call the function `doClick`. However, they each get events during a different stage. The first assignment, using `true` as the last argument, will be fired during the *capture* stage. The second assignment, using `false` as the last argument, will be fired during the *bubble* stage. The default operation if you don't include the last argument is `false` (bubble) stage.

Example of capture vs. bubble

The following example shows how capture and bubble events work. We assign three different handlers to nested div elements; a capture and bubble event on the topmost element, and a bubble event on the innermost element.

HTML

```
<div id="topElem">
  <div id="middleElem">
    <div id="innerElem">
    </div>
  </div>
</div>
```

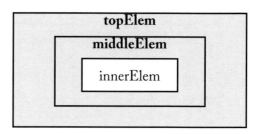

CSS

I included CSS to make the elements look like the above picture:

JavaScript

```
var topElem   = document.getElementById("topElem");
var innerElem = document.getElementById("innerElem");
topElem.addEventListener('click', clickTopBubble, false);
topElem.addEventListener('click', clickTopCapture, true);
innerElem.addEventListener('click', clickInnerBubble, false);
function clickTopBubble(e) {
  console.log("CLICK TOP BUBBLE");
}
function clickTopCapture(e) {
  console.log("CLICK TOP CAPTURE");
}
function clickInnerBubble(e) {
  console.log("CLICK INNER BUBBLE");
}
```

Actions when you click on one of the elements

You can see how events travel down from the top firing capture events, then bubble back up firing bubble events. In any of the sequences below, you could include a stopPropagation (or cancelBubble for IE8) call to stop any further propagation of that event.

- ◆ Click on innerElem fires:
    1. topElem capture event
    2. innerElem bubble event
    3. topElem bubble event
- ◆ Click on middleElem fires:
    1. topElem capture event
    2. topElem bubble event
- ◆ Click on topElem fires:
    1. topElem bubble event
    2. topElem capture event

NOTE: You notice that the last behavior when clicking on the top element seems counter-intuitive to the expected operation. This element acts differently because it is the top level element. The bubble event happens first because it was declared first with the addEventListener method before the capture event in your JavaScript code. If you reverse the order of the addEventListener declarations, then the capture event will fire first in the last example above.

Event delegation using event bubbling

Event bubbling allows you to set one event handler on an outer element that will get all events fired on all inner elements. This helps you greatly reduce the number of handlers in your code. Rather than setting a handler on every row or cell in a table, for example, you can set one handler on the table that will get all events from all the rows. All you will need to do then is check for the id of the element that created the event and take the appropriate action. Elements that you don't recognize will have their events ignored, or you can cancel them.

When you place your handler on the outermost element, you normally will need to know which inner element was acted upon. Your handler can access two properties that will help you properly handle the event:

- `this`: refers to the current element that is handling the event that may have bubbled up from a lower element. It does NOT refer to the element that was initially acted upon. You will have to test for this in another way.

- `target`: you can access the original element that was acted upon by using the following line of code that handles the differences between browsers. The results of this assignment are the same in every handler that is executed when the event bubbles up. You can use this variable to determine the ID of the element that was selected.

```
var target = event.target || event.srcElement;
```

NOTE: The IE `attachEvent` method does not pass any value for `this`.

Delegating events like focus and blur

Some events do not bubble up to outer elements so trying to use a regular event delegation handler will not work. These events include `focus`, `blur`, and `change`. However, these events can be handled by a `capture` handler set up with `addEventListener`. This could be used to know when any child element has received focus, for example.

Differences in event names

The exact name used to assign event handlers varies slightly by browser and by usage. For example, to add a handler that takes care of mouse `click` events, you could use one of the following methods:

```
1.  <div onclick="doThis()">
2.  element.onclick = doThis;
3.  element.addEventListener('click', doThis, false);
4.  element.attachEvent('onclick', doThis); (IE 8 and before)
```

Note that you use `onclick` in all cases except when using `addEventListener`. The same difference applies to other events, such as: `focus/onfocus`, `blur/onblur`, and `keyup/onkeyup`. You will need to test for the proper handlers in your code before you assign them to your handlers.

Setting handlers for mousemove events

You may need to set up an event handler to allow a user to move an element like a slider or small window across the screen. This will involve setting three handlers:

◆ `mousedown`: to capture the starting location of the mouse and set up the `mousemove` and `mouseup` events.

◆ `mousemove`: tracks the mouse location and moves the element appropriately usually using information from the `mousedown` event to know how far to move the element.

◆ `mouseup`: indicates the move event is over and removes the `mousemove` event so that the element doesn't keep moving as you move the mouse without the mouse button depressed.

When you set up these events, you need to be careful to handle cases where the user either quickly moves the mouse, or moves the mouse beyond the location that you actually allow the element to appear. If you assign all three events to the same, original element, you will usually have problems with the mouseup event never firing to stop moving the element. The correct way to assign these handlers is:

1.   Assign the mousedown event handler to the original element that you want to move.

2.   In this mousedown event handler, you need to record the location of the mouse and the location of the element so you can properly move it in the mousemove event handler.

3.   In the mousedown event handler, you also need to assign a mousemove event handler but on an upper level element, usually the document. This ensures you will properly track mouse movement. This handler will reposition the element based on the mouse movement.

4.   In the mousedown event handler, you also will assign the mouseup event handler to the same upper level element or document. The mouseup handler will remove both the mousemove and mouseup handlers (see below for how to remove handlers.)

Removing event handlers

The method of removing event handlers depends on how you created them in the first place. A common reason to remove handlers is handling mousemove events where you need to remove your mousemove and mouseup event handlers when you are done with the move. The methods include:

◆ `detachEvent('click', doThis)`. Use to remove handlers added with the `attach-Event` method (IE 8 and before).

◆ `removeEventListener('click', doThis, true)`. Use to remove handlers added with the `addEventListener` method. You need to match the same third argument used when creating the handler. If you added handlers for both capture and bubble stages, you need to remove each handler separately.

◆ `element.onclick=null`. Use to remove handlers added with `element.onclick=doThis;`

Handling dblClick events

You need to be careful when assigning handlers for `dblClick` events. You would normally add a handler for the `dblclick` event (`ondblclick`) on the element the user will double click on. If you add additional handlers for related events, such as mousedown, mouseup, and click events, you will see the following handlers fired when you double click on the element:

1. `mousedown`
2. `mouseup`
3. `click`
4. `mousedown`
5. `mouseup`
6. `click`
7. `dblclick`

Disabling events on all elements on the screen

There are many times that you want to disable all events on the screen to prevent a user from clicking on active elements while processing is going on. There are a number of ways to do this including setting a variable that all action methods check before executing. There are other ways to accomplish this by setting up a DOM element that covers the entire screen that will accept all events while you are processing the action. To set this up:

* Add a `<div>` element to your DOM so that it is on top of all other elements (set a very high `z-index` property). You can set its `color` and `opacity` properties so that it will dim out the entire screen. When you need to disable all events, simply set its `visibility` property to 'visible'.

Getting the event properties you want

The event object has a number of properties that can be used in your handler. However, starting with the event itself, different browsers handle some of these properties differently. The most common properties you might be interested in include:

* **event**: Some older browsers don't always pass in the event into your handler. You should handle this in each of your handlers in a manner similar to the following:
    ```
    function doSomething(event) {
      event = event || window.event;
    }
    ```
* **target element:** Again, this property is handled differently across browsers. You can include the following line in each handler to ensure you get the proper target object.
    ```
    var target = event.target || event.srcElement;
    ```
* **key code**: Getting the key that was pressed usually consists of two steps. You get the numerical code first, then convert that to a character if you need to, similar to:
    ```
    function keyHandler(event) {
      event    = event || window.event;
      var kcode = event.keyCode || event.which;
      var kchar = String.fromCharCode(kcode);
    }
    ```

A few gotchas here. If you hold a key down, you should get a `keydown` event followed by a keypress event repeating until you release the key which results in a final `keyup` event. Another problem is the code returned by each type of key handler. Let's say you press a lower case 'a' on the keyboard. This character is normally represented by ASCII code 97. However, using the code in the above `keyHandler` function, you will see the following code and characters:

- `keydown:   65 A`
- `keypress: 97 a`
- `keyup:     65 A`

If you pressed a dollar sign (shift-4), you will see the following:

- `keydown:   16`
- `keydown:   52 4`
- `keypress: 36 $`
- `keyup:     52 4`
- `keyup:     16`

The extra `keydown` and `keyup` events for code=16 are for the shift key. Each handler can also query the state of special keys, like `alt`, `ctrl` and `shift` using the following properties:

- event.altKey
- event.ctrlKey
- event.shiftKey

So what do you do? It depends on what you need to capture. If you need the exact character that was entered, you need to either use the `keypress` handler or check the status of the `shiftKey` property in the `keydown` or `keyup` handler and convert the code. Trying to check for special characters gets a little harder especially between operating systems and browsers. For some special keys, you may need to use the `keydown` or `keyup` handler. Be sure to test your implementation on different systems and browsers.

- **mouse button**: You may need to add code to your mouse event handlers to determine which mouse button was being depressed. You normally would ignore right mouse button events. Normal events would be using the left mouse button. You can check for this using code similar to the following which should work on most browsers:

```
function mouseHandler(event) {
  event     = event || window.event;
  var wcode = event.which || event.button;
  if (wcode != 1) return false;      //1=left mouse button
}
```

However there are a few more gotchas for something that should be simple. This method really only works reliably on a `mousedown` or `mouseup` event handler. Checking in a `keypress` handler may not give you consistent results. Plus, a right mouse button click returns different codes for `e.which` and `e.button` so you need to have a different check for those:

```
event.which  = 3
event.button = 2
```

And clicking down on the mouse scroll button (if your mouse has one) returns:

```
event.which  = 2
event.button = 1
```

- **mouse location**: Determining the correct mouse position is also fraught with peril. There are a number of properties you can query in your mouse handlers but you need to understand how each one works. You have to allow for location inside an element and any scrolling that has taken place. And not all browsers support every property. In general, the properties have the following meanings (these are for the horizontal location -- substitute **Y** for **X** to get the vertical location):
  - **clientX**: location relative to window
  - **layerX**: location relative to current element
  - **offsetX**: location relative to current element
  - **pageX**: location relative to window
  - **screenX**: location relative to entire screen
  - **x**: location relative to window

You may need to create one function that will return the position of the mouse on different browsers. It may look something like:

```
function getPosition(e) {
  e = e || window.event;
  var pos = {};
  if (e.pageX) {
    pos.x = e.pageX;
    pos.y = e.pageY;
  } else {
    pos.x = e.clientX + document.body.scrollLeft +
            document.documentElement.scrollLeft;
    pos.y = e.clientY + document.body.scrollTop +
            document.documentElement.scrollTop;
  }
  return pos;
}
```

Summary

Best usage is probably:

1. Add a utility function that handles stopBubble or stopPropagation in one call

2. Use addEventListener to add your event listeners. It is better to separate assigning handlers from HTML code anyway and this method has more flexibility.

3. Decide if having capture events will help organize your code. If so, add this option to the addEventListener methods you call.

4. If you need to stop propagation or prevent the default action, explicitly call these from your methods using stopPropagation and/or preventDefault.

"The best programmers are not marginally better than merely good ones. They are an order-of-magnitude better, measured by whatever standard: conceptual creativity, speed, ingenuity of design, or problem-solving ability."

- Randall E. Stross

8
Handling Data Efficiently

You often have to handle large lists of items that need to be sorted, scrolled, and filtered. This includes lists of names, lists of tv shows, or any other large collection of data that users have to access. There are many ways to handle these operations, but the larger the list, the more you have to pay attention to optimizing memory and performance. The better a job you do, the more data you can handle.

The main tasks that you need to be concerned with include:

- Managing server requests
- Managing memory
- Managing the DOM
- Improving performance, including scrolling, sorting, and filtering

We'll look at each of these areas in detail.

Managing server requests

One of the first design tasks concerns the availability of the data from your servers and how quickly it can be fetched. This is usually a fairly complicated question as it involves a number of considerations based mainly on the size of the dataset, the frequency that it changes, and the end use of the data. Questions you should ask include:

- Does the dataset have to be created each time it is requested using database queries or is it fairly static data that changes infrequently? What if changes just once a day?

- How many servers are available and what is their capacity? What kind of caching is available?

- How many concurrent users will be using your application? How frequently will they need to request new data?

- Can the data be broken down into smaller sets so each user doesn't need to fetch as much each time?

- Can you break the data down into lookup tables so that the main dataset can be smaller and simply reference data in the table?

- Are requests from multiple users or even from the same user cacheable? Do they have the same URL or is each request unique?

There are other considerations that may be unique to your application and server installation. I worked on software for set-top boxes in Europe that would fetch large amounts of TV data every time the boxes started. Unfortunately, at the time, there were frequent power outages in the area resulting in all boxes coming online and requesting data at exactly the same time. We had to add some randomizing timing code to prevent all the requests from happening at the same time.

Another TV application I worked on was originally set up to request data from the server in very verbose segments that required almost 200MB of data fetches to populate a TV guide. By reworking the data structure into a compact format with lookup tables, I was able to reduce the total payload to 3MB that loaded almost instantly. So be creative and look at all facets of your project for ways to optimize its performance. It may seem that you don't need to worry about bandwidth, transmission speed, and memory but you should try to design your application with these factors in mind.

Don't let the server make UI decisions for you

Don't let the server API's, size of the data payload, or data format affect how the UI displays data. Make sure the data received from the server is in the optimal format for the application so it doesn't have to be sorted or manipulated prior to use. This includes getting a date field in a format-free value such as milliseconds or a JSON date format that can be directly converted by your JavaScript code. That way you can display the date in whatever format you need or even let the user decide which date format to use. It is also easier to sort.

Managing memory and bandwidth

Managing memory can be more complicated than managing your server requests. Decreasing your bandwidth with smaller data objects from the server often will reduce your memory use as well but that depends on the exact format of the objects you receive from the server. Different browsers handle memory in different ways and it is hard to know exactly how users will be using your application. Computers have more memory than before but you still have mobile devices that are more limited. And you are usually not the only application running on the device. I think the best approach is to design your memory usage carefully up front, then keep everything as small as possible at each step of your development. Some things to keep in mind:

- Keep your data structures as lean as possible with only the fields that you need. Arrays may save space compared to objects. Keep your property names short. Having shorter variable and property names mainly affects the size of the files that must be downloaded. The effect of shorter names on actual code performance is very small since names are essentially changed to address offsets. Make sure the name is long enough to be descriptive in their context.

- If you have a large dataset, try to make it as relational as possible with lookup tables for common data.

- Only download the data that you need from the server.

- Delete functions, arrays, and objects that you no longer need. Remember that you can't control or force garbage collection in JavaScript. It may happen at a time when you least expect it, such as during fast scrolling. So avoid creating the garbage in the first place.

- Watch your usage of graphic images. Try to design your screens so that most of the major graphical elements are reused as much as possible. Use solid colors or font characters instead of graphical images.

- Use lazy loading of code, data, and graphics as much as possible. This means you delay loading of items until you need them or until the user has accessed a function in the program that requires them. This is often done to enable you to show the opening screen as fast as possible by delaying loading of secondary material.

Managing the DOM

The size and makeup of your DOM will also impact your memory usage and performance. This mainly comes into play when you have a single-page application that has to display a lot of data, such as scrolling lists of items. The bigger your DOM, the more memory is used and the slower your UI navigation becomes. If you have a fairly simple interface, then you normally don't have to worry to much about the complexity of the DOM. However, things you should be aware of when displaying large amounts of data include:

- Reuse elements of your DOM as much as possible. If you have a number of screens that have similar backgrounds, use one common background with different elements on top.

- Avoid thrashing the DOM. Don't keep adding and deleting elements in your HTML. Layout is expensive and even simple tasks like querying an element's position can be slow.

- Set an element's `display` property to `none` if you don't need to show it now but will need it later. Be aware that may change a page's appearance since other elements might change position as a result, so be sure you design your pages to avoid this problem. A common use would be an application that contains a main menu with buttons that display separate elements, perhaps by sliding them on and off the screen. Once you slide an element off the screen, you can set its `display` property to `none`. To redisplay this element, set its `display` property to `block` before sliding it back on the screen.

- Keep your HTML as 'light' as possible by:
  - Avoid extra elements if possible, such as nested `spans` and `divs`.
  - Minimize the use of special effects like drop shadows, text shadows, and gradients.
  - Avoid transparency if possible, particularly if you are moving elements across the screen. Text has to be anti-aliased against the background as it is moved.
  - Be careful using `transitions` and `transforms` as they can impact performance. Some animations will be accelerated by the hardware so you should use those methods as much as possible. In general, performance will suffer as you increase the number and/or size of the elements you are moving or resizing.
  - Some seemingly simple effects can have negative performance results, such as rotating text.

- Keep your CSS as simple as possible. I try to avoid grouping and nesting my CSS selectors as it can be slow and confusing. The browser has to resolve the nesting behavior and if you are not careful, this can take time. Plus, I have found excessive nesting makes it harder to maintain the code and make specific changes to an element. Use it only when you need it.

- Keep HTML comments to a minimum or ensure they are removed before generating the final application.

Improving performance

If you have properly handled the previous goals for handling server requests, memory usage, and DOM design, then you have already done most of the work for improving your application's performance. However, there are probably still areas where you can improve the real or perceived performance of your application when dealing with large amounts of data. Pay attention to the *perceived* performance which is essentially how the user thinks the application is performing. Little things like giving immediate feedback and filling in some of the screen right away can go a long way to making the app look and feel better. Areas to consider include:

- Sometimes you may want to load all your program files and data when the program starts so that your performance will be faster later in the program. You normally want to make sure that you display some UI right away with some indication that you are loading data. If your user will be using your application for some time, a little extra time up front will be worth it for better performance elsewhere. You can defer loading some items, such as help screens, until they are actually requested. Users are accustomed to waiting a bit longer to display these types of items. By keeping your code as small as possible and avoiding loading large libraries or frameworks, you will have more memory for your data and UI.

- Show a progress meter or spinner whenever your application is carrying out a function that may take more than a second or so. If it is a lengthy task, you may want to display more information about what you are doing, such as: 'Calculating totals...' However, you have to be careful about displaying the progress of calculations in programming loops since you normally have to interrupt the loop using something like a setTimeout command to allow the UI to display the updated message. This alone will slow down your application. If you do display a message, try to use the innerText property of the element to avoid a DOM reflow.

- Give immediate feedback whenever the user clicks on any control in your UI. This is very important and often overlooked. This can range from just having a button move or change color to having a new screen display. Show a gray overlay over the entire screen if you don't want the user to interact with your interface while you are changing the page.

- Don't mess with the DOM. Minimize the number of times you destroy or create parts of the DOM. Minimize the number of times you have to reflow the DOM by requesting values such as offsetLeft, offsetTop, and similar properties.

Real life examples

I have worked on several applications that handled very large datasets that had to be loaded from the server and manipulated by the UI. The design and programming went through several iterations as it had its memory footprint reduced and its performance improved. One big advantage I had was that I could change the format of the data that was requested. This may not always be possible but being able to change the data structure is usually critical to your optimization efforts.

A TV programming guide

I wrote a mobile application for a large TV cable company that displayed their entire TV schedule for two weeks in a scrolling grid similar to guides you see on your television. This project was a case of having to optimize the code in 3 areas—payload size, memory usage, and performance. It involved reading their schedule data using server API calls when the application started. The original design called for requesting the data in 3-hour chunks and *stitching* the events together in the UI code. This was done using JSON requests that returned data similar to the following. Each 3-hour segment contained all shows that were on during that period, even if only for a few minutes. Each segment contained information for approximately 2000 shows that aired at some point during those 3 hours. The structure looked similar to:

```
{
"shows": [
  "show": {
    "title":          "Raiders of the Lost Ark",
    "type":           "Movie",
    "rating":         "TV-14",
    "resolution":     "HD",
    "startTime":      "2012-04-23T18:00:00.000Z",
    "endTime";        "2012-04-23T18:30:00.000Z",
    "duration":       30,
    "channelID":      12,
    "channelName":    "CSPAN"
    },
  "show": { ....etc.
  ]
}
```

The choices for some of the fields are:

* type: Movie, Sports, Kids, News
* resolution: HD, SD
* rating: "NA", "TV-Y", "TV-Y7", "NR(General)", "G/TV-G", "PG/TV-PG", "PG-13", "TV-14", "TV-MA", "R", "NC-17", "NR(Adult)"

The schedule covered hundreds of channels for fourteen days, so the number of shows requested was very large. The first step was to go over the requirements for the application:

* The grid was to display all channels and be able to scroll for two weeks.
* The primary target platform was a mobile device so the data transmitted should be as small as possible.

- The app should start working as soon as possible, at least showing some shows for the current time period.
- The data could be pre-processed on the server into whatever format I needed.
- The channel lineup (list of channels) would change infrequently and only at night. There may be updates to a specific show during the day which would have to be picked up by the application.

So I began to analyze and change the data one section at a time. Some of this required analyzing the data on the server to look for areas that could be optimized.

Step 1 - Dates: The date format seemed very lengthy so I had it changed to a milliseconds time representation that could be converted directly with JavaScript's `new Date()` function. So now the dates looked like the following, which was both smaller and would convert to a JavaScript date slightly faster in the app:

```
"startTime": 1335204000000,
"endTime";   1335205800000,
```

Step 2 - Duration: Since I had a start and end date, I could delete the `duration` field.

Step 3 - Title: This took a little bit of analysis of the data on the server. There were over 150,000 airings of shows but many of the show titles were the same due to reruns and multiple airings. Once I sorted all the titles and removed the duplicates, I ended up with a list of several thousand unique names. I created an array of these titles and then added an index reference to the show information instead of the full title. This saved a huge amount of data. I had two choices when making this file:

- Order the title list by most frequent title first since the most common reference number would then be a shorter 1 or 2 digit number instead of a longer 3-4 digit number; or
- Order the list alphabetically. This had the added advantage of being able to use this ordered list in the user interface to display a list of all shows without having to resort the list. This is the option I chose.

Step 4- Channel ID/Name: Since the channel lineup changed very infrequently, this could also be made into a lookup table with each show record containing an index into the table.

Now a show record looks like the following (along with the lookup tables for show titles and channel names):

```
"show": {
  "title":      12,
  "type":       "Movie",
  "rating":     "TV-14",
  "resolution": "HD",
  "startTime":  1335204000000,
  "endTime";    1335205800000,
  "chanIdx":    8
  },
```

Step 5 - Show properties: This one was a little harder. There were three properties that were each set from a small number of possibilities—type, rating, and resolution. This made them prime candidates for using a *bitwise operator* to represent the values. A bitwise operator essentially uses every bit of a number (up to 31 bits) as a true/false flag for the value at that position. Thus, the first bit may represent `type=Movie`, the second bit `type=Sports,` and so on. There are several ways to set and read these values, but the simplest is to use the `&` and `|` operators. You create a number variable set to zero and then use the *or* operator (`|`) to turn on the bits you want.

```
var flag = 0;
flag|=Math.pow(2,5);   //turns on (sets to 1) the 6th bit in flag
flag|=Math.pow(2,8);   //turns on 9th bit, leaving the other bits alone
```

To test the values of the variable flag, you can use code similar to:

```
if (flag&Math.pow(2,5)) { //do true function here for 6th bit true}
```

I used this method to combine all three fields (type, rating, and resolution) into one flag field.

Now, the data looks like:

```
"show": {
  "title":    12,
  "flag":     16823,              //bitwise number
  "startTime": 1335204000000,
  "endTime";   1335205800000,
  "chanIdx":  8
  },
```

Step 6- Combining all shows per channel: This also took some analysis of the data on the server and how the data was assembled before being transmitted to the application. This included:

• I discovered that shows for each channel were always contiguous meaning there were no gaps in the schedule—when one show ended, the next show in the list started. This allowed me to further compress the data since I no longer needed start AND end time for each show.

• I also realized that I didn't need the millisecond accuracy from the `startTime` property, nor even second accuracy—accuracy to the nearest minute was more than sufficient to display the program grid or information about a selected show.

• I could also make the start time fields smaller by using a start time offset based on the start time of the entire grid. Thus, if the 14-day grid started Monday morning, I could just send the date representation for this time, and then make all the start times for all shows be simply minute offsets from this time. Thus, the field length went down from 13 bytes to 1-5 bytes.

• The final reason for combining shows was that relying on 3-hour self-contained segments meant that almost 30% of the shows were repeated in the next 3-hour segment since they spanned the 3 hour boundary. Having one list of continuous shows per channel removed this duplication.

For various reasons, I decided to separate the show data into several arrays rather than either one set of objects or multi-level arrays. These made for smaller payloads, smaller memory usage, and slightly faster access times. Properties at the same location in each array were for the same show. So now, the data looked like (with all numbers for each channel in each array element):

```
"titles":          ["Angels", "Armada", "As the World Turns", ..
"chans":           [[2, "KRON"], [4, "KPIX"], ...
"gridStartTime:    1335205800000,
"showTitles":      [[23, 211, 3, 6,...], [6541, 12, 22...
"showFlags":       [[345, 1244, 1122, ...], [233, 12, 1122, ...
"showTimes":       [[0, 30, 60, ...], [0, 90, 180...
```

The original plan using 3-hour segments took a long time to load and needed almost 200MB of data being transmitted. The new format downloaded almost immediately and used only around 4MB of memory.

Updating: The entire database would be downloaded each day by any application that was still running. Any new instance of the application would always get the latest data when it started. Since the data was essentially the same for all users in any given area that had the same channel lineup, it could be pre-built and cached in multiple places. Updates during the day involving changes for a specific shows were handled by:

- Each application making a very lightweight call to the server periodically asking for updates, if any.

- Updates were returned by sending just the array elements for the channels that had changes. These would simply replace the existing array member (not the entire array) and the UI was refreshed if needed. Changes to the actual show title could be handled by either sending the entire title array again, or simply appending a new title to the end. This would result in the title list not be completely alphabetical but this would be corrected the next time the complete data was loaded.

Scrolling, sorting, and filtering large lists

I designed several applications that had to scroll very large lists of data while allowing the user to quickly sort and filter the displayed list. I had to make the sorting and filtering operation as fast as possible and also allow for smooth scrolling on PC's and mobile devices. For various reasons, I wanted to load the entire list once and then handle all the operations in the application without having to make further server requests. If you design it correctly, you should be able to make this work for tens of thousands of records giving the user a much better experience than typical *'load ten at a time'* browsing. Obviously, the requirements will vary by application. If only the top 30 records of data you retrieve will be of interest (similar to a search engine request), then some of these techniques will not be needed. However, if you want to be able to retrieve data, change a filter, resort it on different fields, then these methods apply. The areas I focused on included:

- Making the data format loaded from the server as small and efficient as possible.

- Loading the data into one large array that is not changed when filtering or sorting. This will help cut down on garbage creation and be more efficient.

- Building separate arrays of indexes for each sort order when requested. These arrays will be in the requested order but are simply pointers into the main data array. These could also be pre-built and downloaded from the server.

- Adding a filter flag to each array member that is set to true or false whenever the filter is changed. This way the filter code does not have to be rerun every time the sort order changes.

- Keeping the DOM footprint as small as possible. This involved make the elements displaying the data as lightweight as possible and setting the `display` property to `none` for elements that were not currently displayed.

Step 1 - Data format

Start with making your data format as compact as possible. I loaded my data as a JSON array object with only the fields that I needed. I made sure the data was created on the server in the initial sort order that I wanted, in this case alphabetically by name. This assumes that the dataset is small enough to be fetched and displayed in its entirety. If the data is just too large, you will have to load it in pieces as the user scrolls through the list. All of the concepts mentioned here can be used even for lists loaded in sections. However, if you are displaying a partial list in a large `div` using the scrollbars (instead of a next/prev type button), you may want to set the height of the containing `div` element to the full height as if all of the rows were loaded to ensure that the scroll bar looks and acts correctly.

Step 2 - Display of data

To allow for optimal sorting and filtering, I usually lay out the data by placing the data fields inside a `<div>` element for each row, using absolute position for each row. I increment a row height counter to set the `top` property of each row. Each row is identified with a unique ID that directly references the array element index of the data. Try to keep the HTML elements as 'light' as possible. This means to avoid nesting a lot of elements in each row and keep CSS effects to a minimum—no shadows, transforms, or images for example.

Step 3 - Adding sort

Now add the ability to sort the table on any of the columns. You would add some method to display the current sort column and let the user change that order. This is usually done by clicking on the column header to change the order which is then shown by a small triangle icon. Then create a new array of indexes in this new sort order that points to your original data array. This minimizes the amount of data you have to move around and you can keep the sort index array to use again if the user resorts on this column. If the user specifies a reverse sort, you can use the same index array in the opposite order.

Step 4 - Filtering

Now add the ability to filter the list. This has a few components.

1. First, create a screen that allows the user to select the fields and values they wish to filter on.

2. Then, using the filter criteria, walk through all the data records setting a filter flag to true or false. You want to set it once so it doesn't have to be run again if the sort order is changed.

3. Now, using the current sort order array, you want to walk through each row `<div>` element which you can directly reference by ID. If the filter flag is true, you can set the display property to 'block'; otherwise, set it to 'none'. This will remove it from the DOM tree. At the same time, you will set the `top` property of the element to position it in order. By just hiding and moving existing DOM elements, you reduce the amount of DOM thrashing and avoid deleting and creating a lot of elements.

Step 5 - Scrolling large lists

Your list of `<div>` elements elements can be placed inside one large <div> that has the `overflow` property set to `auto` or `scroll`. Then, size this outside element to always fit on your page. This allows you to keep other elements (like menus or column headers) always visible on the page. Unless the list is large, you can usually display all the rows in your list. However, for very large lists, you may need to limit the number of `div` elements that are actually visible in the DOM (`display=block`) at one time. Having too many elements displayed at one time will slow down your scrolling and screen transitions.

One way to handle this problem is to add a handler on the scroll event for the parent `div` element of your list. In that handler, you can detect the location of the scroll bar, and, using the height of each row and the height of the window, determine which elements are currently being displayed. You can then set the `display` property of those rows to 'block' while setting all the other row's `display` property to 'none'. To make the next page up or down scrolling a little smoother, you may wish to set the display property of the 100 rows above and below the currently visible row to `block` as well.

Caching

Caching your server requests makes your data loading go faster as copies of the data that exist in either your local cache or server cache can be used. The downside is that you may get 'stale' data that has since been changed on the server. This includes new versions of program files or data that may be frequently changed on the server. Most applications use some kind of 'cache busting' technique to ensure that they always load the latest file. The downside is that it will always make the program and data load more slowly. A frequent method is to append a timestamp to the end of each url request to force the url to appear to be a new request that will bypass any cache. Using something like a JavaScript date object displayed in milliseconds is often used.

However, you may find that neither the data nor the program changes that often (but it does change.) If that is the case, you could try using a timestamp for your cache busting that only changes once a day (or some similar interval.) This will at least allow some caching for all accesses during that day.

Sometimes you may have large data sets that you want to be cached on the server or edge servers for use by many users. If so, you may need to ensure that all the requests for that data look the same. This means not including a user ID with each request, for example. For some of the TV guide programs I worked on, this was solved by having the show data fetched with one generic call, while a second call that included a user ID and location was made that returned any personalized information about those shows. The application then combined those two files together in the browser code.

"There is no programming language—no matter how structured—that will prevent programmers from making bad programs."

-Larry Flon

9

Fetching Server Data

Your applications will most likely be accessing a server to store and retrieve data, settings, or images. There are a number of factors you need to be aware of when writing applications that have to access a server other than the initial loading of your JavaScript, HTML, and CSS files.

Using *GET* or *POST* requests

You will normally use either a GET or a POST request to communicate with your servers. There are some significant differences between these methods that you need to be aware of when designing your application.

GET

This method is normally used to request data from the server. However, you can also include data in the request that the server can save. Some points about GET requests:

- ◆ **Format**: The request consists of two parts: the URL, and the name/value pairs of the required data. The first data pair is preceded by a question mark (?). Any other pairs are preceded by an ampersand (&). The request looks like: `http://xx.yy.com/app/?name1=val1&name2=val2`. Only ASCII characters can be sent. Note: you should include the final slash (/) before the question mark to be correct. It may also make a difference with some SEO routines.

- ◆ **Caching**: These requests can be cached (see comments below about JSONP requests).

- ◆ **Bookmarking**: Since everything is contained in the request string, GET requests can be saved and bookmarked for later use.

- ◆ **Visibility**: Any data contained in the request are easily visible to the user.

- ◆ **Size**: Get requests have a maximum length which varies by browser and server but it is usually around 2048 characters.

POST

This method is normally used to save data to the server, often from fields filled in on an HTML form. Some points about POST requests:

- ◆ **Format**: The request consists of the URL. The name/value pairs are send in the message body. Binary data can be sent.

- ◆ **Caching**: These requests are not cached.
- ◆ **Bookmarking**: Post requests cannot be bookmarked.
- ◆ **Visibility**: Any data is not displayed in the URL.
- ◆ **Size**: There is no reasonable restriction on the amount of data sent.

Cross-domain problems

You are making cross-domain requests if your code is making GET or POST requests to a server that is in a different domain. Thus, if your app is running on www.sample.com, a request it makes to a server application on www.test.com is a cross domain request. If you need to make these kinds of requests, you have two options:

- ◆ **CORS (Cross-Origin Resource Sharing):** This has to be set up on the server you are referencing so that it will accept requests from your server.
- ◆ **JSONP:** This stands for "JSON with Padding". These requests are made by setting a source property on a script tag which is added to your DOM. Your requesting URL must include a unique name that is used by the server to wrap the returned data inside a function that will be executed by your browser. Thus, a regular JSON object might look like:

```
{
"name":   "John Jones",
"age":    12
}
```

and the corresponding JSONP would look like:

```
cb123({
"name":   "John Jones",
"age":    12
});
```

Your code must create the function that is called by the JSONP before requesting the data (in this case cb123). Be aware that parse errors in the JSONP data may create an uncatchable error. This is usually caused by the server not wrapping the data inside a function call.

NOTE: JSONP can only be used with GET requests and not PUT requests.

Differences between UNIX and Windows

If you are moving or sharing files between UNIX and Windows computers and servers, there are a few differences you should be aware of, including:

- ◆ **Line endings.** UNIX files use just a single LF (line feed) to end lines where Windows uses CRLF (carriage return/line feed). Source control systems usually handle this but you need to be careful.
- ◆ **Character encoding.** Character encodings of special characters may be different between the systems.
- ◆ **Filenames.** UNIX systems normally handle upper and lower case characters differently. Windows systems normally ignore case in file and folder names. To avoid possible problems, I try to keep all folder and file names in lowercase.

Using canned data

If your application relies on data downloaded from the server you may want to consider having this data available locally in pre-built data files. This if often referred to as *canned data* and can be very helpful for several reasons:

1. You often may not have the server API's or data working properly in time for you to use when programming your interface. You want to be able to fill in lists and write the code to properly display the screen the first time instead of having to stub it out now and completely redo it later.

2. You may have to run the program in the future when you do not have proper connections to the server, or the servers are not working for some reason. This can happen when giving demonstrations to management, or at trade shows.

3. It can also be used before the server API's are in place to allow you to design the appropriate JSON data structure and get it completely designed before giving it to the programmer who is implementing the server API.

Limitations

Obviously you cannot recreate all of the server API's using canned data. If your application displays a list of names that allow the user to select any name to fetch detailed information from the server, you obviously will have to have canned data for only one or two names and then add a test mode to your app to indicate when to load only those files. But it can be very helpful for this and other startup data files that are loaded once.

Setting up canned data

Adding the data to your canned data files is fairly straightforward. You have two main choices:

*   If you do not have the server API in place, you will need to manually enter the data in a valid JSON format using a text editor, or

*   If you have the API working but want to guard against it not being available in the future, or maybe it is almost correct, or you want to work offline, you can do something similar to the following (it may change slightly in different browsers):

    1. Before doing these steps, you should add a JSON formatter extension to your browser.

    2. Open your browser and the browser's debug console or developer's tool.

    3. Go to the *network* tab in your debug console.

    4. Load your application and execute the API request you are concerned with, or simply enter the URL in the browser's URL field. If the API has been executed from your program, you can do the following:

        a. In the network tab, you will the requests for all of the files that your application loads, including the data request.

        b. Right click on the name of the API request you want to capture and select the '*Open link in new tab*' option.

        c. A new browser window will open displaying the results of the request. If you have a JSON formatter in your browser, it should be nicely formatted and indented.

        d. Copy and paste this data to a text file and give it an appropriate name.

Once you have the file, there is another decision you need to make in order to format it properly. If it is to be fetched with a regular JSON fetch, you can use it as is. However, if you want it to substitute for a JSONP server request, you have a few more steps. In order for it to be fetched as a JSONP file, the data will have to be wrapped inside a function call with a name known to the application. One way to accomplish this is it:

1. Decide on a unique function name (such as `cbAddressData`) for each file and add that around the data object, similar to the following where `xxxx` represents your regular JSON object:

    `cbAddressData({xxxx});`

2. Append this name as the callback to your JSONP fetch instead of using a randomly generated name. This fetch will fetch your file from your local file system instead of a server.

Validating your JSON files

When entering canned data files manually or testing new server API's, you may need to validate your JSON data to ensure it is formatted correctly and to get a clear idea of what all the fields look like. Some methods to help you do this include:

◆   Install a JSON parser extension to your browser so you can parse JSON files that you fetch to your browser window.

◆   Copy and paste your JSON file into an online JSON validator or parser. There are a number of free tools available that you can find by searching the Internet. These will point out errors like missing quotation marks and improperly formatted fields. If you are trying to validate a JSONP object, your may have to strip out the surrounding function in order for it to be evaluated properly.

Converting between JSON objects and Javascript objects

There are several ways to convert your JSON objects to objects that you can use directly in your JavaScript code.

◆   Built-in `eval` function. This is not recommended as it can convert objects but also execute Javascript code that might be malicious. There are other differences as well between this and the next method.

◆   `JSON.parse`. This method is designed to convert any of your JSON objects directly to JavaScript objects and is the preferred method.

Another method that you will use is `JSON.stringify()` to convert your JavaScript objects directly into a JSON string that can be sent to your server.

Caching your server requests

Caching refers to the method of responding to your requests for data by using the response from an earlier request. This can be used for your program files, image files, or data files using HTTP requests. It can be very helpful when loading the same program files repeatedly every time you run an application. Responses can be cached at various locations in the fetch process, starting with your browser's cache. This reduces the load on the server and increases the responsiveness of your application.

There are a number of factors that affect when caching is used. These include information in HTML file headers and, most importantly, the exact URL request that is sent. You can use this information to help influence when your requests are cached. There are a number of strategies that you can find by doing an online search, many involving the use of `Expires` or `Cache-Control` in your file headers, or the use of entity tags (ETags).

Disabling caching

The most common times you may want to ensure caching is disabled include:

◆ Requesting time sensitive information that may be continually updated on the server so you need to ensure you have the latest information.

◆ Loading program files (HTML, CSS, and JavaScript) for your application when you are developing your application and those files might be frequently changing. A common way to disable caching in this instance is to add a random string, such as the current time in milliseconds, to the filename of each file when requesting them using JavaScript fetches.

◆ Use your browser's 'clear cache' function to manually clear the current cache.

Enabling caching

There are times that you want to ensure that cached data is used, mainly to speed up your application and reduce server load. A few things to remember when trying to do this include:

◆ You can only cache `GET` requests. `POST` requests cannot be cached.

◆ Your requesting URL must be the same as a previous request in order for the response to be cached. You may want to ensure that your data is split up so that as much information can be fetched with identical URL's and that user-specific requests are kept to a minimum. Remember that caching can occur at different locations in the network so requests from different users may be cached as well.

◆ JSONP requests. Routines that make JSONP requests normally attach a unique string to the end of the URL to be used for constructing the callback function which is required for JSONP to work. That unique string will make the request uncacheable. In order to cache these requests, you will need to use the same callback string for each request. You can try varying this string every 12 or 24 hours to ensure you periodically get a fresh copy.

Reduce the amount of data you have to handle

You should try to minimize the amount of data you receive from your servers. This will decrease the load on the server, improve load times, and decrease the amount of memory your application uses. Ways to accomplish this include:

- Keep all field names as short as possible.
- Change filenames if possible to make them easy to reference by index number or a computable name.
- Put all images in one directory structure and send that name once and have your app prepend that name to each filename.
- Don't send unneeded information. Create separate API's that return just what you need or add a method on the API to specify just the fields you need.
- Try to avoid really long ids for your records. Even if you have 100,000 objects, you really only need a string 6 chars long, or even shorter if you hash it a bit.
- Combine binary fields on the server into bit arrays and send just the numbers representing the bits.
- Don't send images in a size any bigger than you need. These large images force the browser to resize them before displaying. Remember that being twice as wide and twice as high results in a file that is up to 4 times bigger.

10
Localization

Localization refers to ensuring that your application adapts to the country, language, customs, or preferences of the user using it. It is easy to forget when writing applications for the U.S. market that some users might be located in different countries or have different preferences. The items that you need to consider for localization include:

- Date format
- Language of the user interface
- Number and time format
- Currency format
- Special text characters and sorting rules
- Significance of icon and colors

You will need to analyze your target audience to determine the amount of localization you need to provide with your application. There are also two methods of localization to consider as well:

1. Start-up localization. You determine the correct formats to use when your application starts and use that for all parts of your app.

2. User-selectable localization. You may determine a default setup when your app starts but have a setup screen where the user can select their desired options for each area of localization. This may require more coding as all the formatting would have to be able to be changed dynamically at any time including whatever is displayed on the screen.

Date format

To allow dynamic changes to the display of dates and times, you may want to add two basic functions to your code:

- **An all-purpose date formatting function.** This will allow you to pass in a date object and a string representing how you want it displayed and have the formatted date returned. See the example code later in this chapter for one way to do this.

- **Specific date/time routines set by user settings.** You should have a common function that is called throughout the app to format date and time. To make these routines as fast as possible, they should be set to optimized routines for the date/time format selected by the user. This will be more efficient than having conditional logic that is run every time you need to format a date or time. You could have a common routine that is called throughout the app called something like:

```
var formatDate = {};
```

Then you could have other functions that are specified to each date format, such as:

```
var formatDateRoutines = [];
formatDateRoutines[0] = function() {
   //code for date format 0
};
formatDateRoutines[1] = function() {
  //code for date format 1
};
```

Then set the formatDate function equal to the appropriate function from the array of functions, similar to:

```
formatDate = formatDateRoutines[1];
```

Working with dates and times

Date objects are relatively costly to create. Try to minimize the number of times you need to create them. Remember that you can use the following methods to set times of a date object. These methods are not always well documented (or remembered.)

```
var ndate  = new Date();      //new date object using now time
ndate.setMinutes(0,0,0);      //sets minutes/seconds/ms
ndate.setHours(0,0,0,0);      //sets hours/minutes/seconds/ms
var ndate2 = new Date(yy, mm, dd, hh, mm, ss, ms); //set date with all
```

Remember that dates are objects so are passed by reference and not by value so you need to be careful that you don't link date objects together unintentionally.

```
var nd  = new Date();
var nd2 = nd;
nd.setHours(0, 0, 0, 0);          //this changes value of nd and nd2
```

If you need a new date object based on existing one, you can do something like:

```
var nd3 = new Date(nd.getTime()); //this creates new date object
```

To calculate a new date based on an existing date, you can simply add or subtract the appropriate number of milliseconds and then create a new date object, similar to:

```
var a       = new Date();
var numDays = 9;
var b       = new Date(a.getTime()+(numDays * 24 * 60 * 60000));
```

Date function to update time every minute

Making new Date objects is costly in terms of time and can often be done unnecessarily. Often, you do not need a date object that is accurate to the second or millisecond. There are times that you do which is fine, but I am talking about more common uses like displaying the time on the screen. An easy solution is to have one routine that is fired every minute that sets a global time object with correct values and calls back any registered functions with the new time so they can update their display.

```
//global object with latest time values
nowTime =   {
     obj:    new Date(),
     ms:     0,
     mins:   0,
     day:    0
};
var timerMinute      = null;    //set to timeout for each minute
var minuteTimer = function() {
     clearTimeout(timerMinute);
     nowTime.obj       = new Date();
     nowTime.ms        = nowTime.obj.getTime();
     var mdate         = nowTime.obj.getDate();   //day of month
     var newDay        = (mdate != nowTime.day) ? true : false;
     nowTime.day       = mdate;
     notifyListeners(nowTime, newDay);     //notify callbacks
     var nsecs         = (60 - nowTime.obj.getSeconds()) * 1000;
     timerMinute       = setTimeout(function(){minuteTimer();},nsecs);
};
minuteTimer();     //START MINUTE TIMER
```

Using icons and colors

You may be using special icons to indicate things like OK, Stop, Warning, or similar situations. Just be aware that icons that make sense in the United States, such as a stop sign or checkmark, may have different meanings, or no meanings, in other countries or cultures.

The same problem may arise with the use of colors, like red and green, to indicate things like bad or good. You need to ensure that the usage will not have the opposite meaning, and that you have other means of indicating the meaning in addition to the color. You also may need to consider how visible your selected colors are to color-blind users. If you are relying on colors for indicating selections or emphasis, you may want to include an Options section where the user can select which color combinations they want.

Date and time formatting functions

The code below is an example library routine that can convert dates and numbers to a display-able string based on a 'mask' that you pass in along with the string to convert. The functions are wrapped in an object (xFormat). The arrays and values at the top of the object for weekday names, month names, and decimal/comma separators should be set and changed to reflect the current language and country preferences.

To format a date:

```
var newstr = xFormat.formatDate(dateobj, mask);


obj  = date object or null to use today's date
mask = string of characters from list below. Any character not listed
       is returned in the formatted string, such as / separators
       Example: "mm/dd/yy hh:nn am"
//     n nn: minutes
//     h hh: hours (12 hour)  H HH: hours (24 hour)
//     am: am or pm   a:a or p  (app can ucase it if they want)
//     d: day of month   dd: zero filled   ddd: Sun  dddd: Sunday
//     m: month number   mm: zero filled   mmm: Feb  mmmm: February
//     yy: 12    yyyy: 2012
```

To format a number:

```
var n = xFormat.formatNumberObj(num, mask);


num  = number to format
mask = string of characters from list below. Include a special
       character in any place to invoke that display in the proper place
       Example: '$R#,#.#'
//     $:  dollar sign at start
//     R:  make number red if negative
//     G:  make number green if positive
//     ,:  put comma between thousands (you can also use C)
//     .:  put period in front of decimal place
//     +-: put plus or minus in front of number
//     #:  represents a number, you only need one for the whole number
//         used after period indicates how many decimal points
//     (:  put parenthesis around negative numbers
//     %:  put percent symbol at end of number
```

Sample functions

```
var xFormat = {
  weekdayNamesLong:  ["Sunday", "Monday", "Tuesday", "Wednesday",
    "Thursday", "Friday", "Saturday"],
  weekdayNamesShort: ["Sun", "Mon", "Tue", "Wed", "Thu", "Fri", "Sat"],
  monthNamesLong:    ["January", "February", "March", "April", "May",
    "June", "July", "August", "September", "October", "November",
    "December"],
  monthNamesShort:   ["Jan", "Feb", "Mar", "Apr", "May", "Jun", "Jul",
    "Aug", "Sep", "Oct", "Nov", "Dec"],
  strDec:            '.',
  strThou:           ',',

  formatDate: function(obj, mask) {
    obj = (this.isDate(obj)) ? obj : (obj) ? (new Date(obj)):(new Date());
    return this.formatTimeDate(mask,
      obj.getMinutes(),
```

```
      obj.getHours(),
      obj.getDate(),
      obj.getDay(),
      obj.getMonth(),
      obj.getUTCFullYear());
},

isDate: function(obj) {
  return Object.prototype.toString.call(obj) === '[object Date]';
},

formatTimeDate: function(str, mins, hrs, mdate, wday, mon, yr) {
  var ampm    = '';
  var hrzero  = '';

  //REPLACE YEAR
  str = str.replace("yyyy",yr);
  str = str.replace("yy",(yr%100));

  //REPLACE MONTH DATE
  var dayzero = (mdate < 10) ? "0" : "";
  str = str.replace("dddd", "xxxx");
  str = str.replace("ddd",  "xxx");
  str = str.replace("dd",   dayzero + mdate);
  str = str.replace("d",    mdate);

  //MINUTES
  var minszero = (mins < 10) ? "0" : "";
  str = str.replace("nn",minszero + mins);
  str = str.replace("n",mins);

   //HOURS
  if (str.indexOf("H") >= 0) {
    hrzero = (hrs < 10) ? "0" : "";
    str    = str.replace("HH",hrzero + hrs);
    str    = str.replace("H",hrs);
  } else {
    ampm = "am";
    if (hrs >= 12) {
      hrs  =  (hrs > 12) ? (hrs-12) : hrs;
      ampm = "pm";
    }
    hrzero = (hrs < 10) ? "0" : "";
    str    = str.replace("hh",hrzero + hrs);
    str    = str.replace("h",hrs);
  }
```

```
    //12 HOUR CLOCK
    str = str.replace("am","zz");
    str = str.replace("a","z");

    //MONTH (do last so it doesn't change any 'am' in the string
    var monzero = (mon < 9) ? "0" : "";
    str = str.replace("mmmm", "zzzz");
    str = str.replace("mmm",  "zzz");
    str = str.replace("mm",   monzero + (mon+1));
    str = str.replace("m",    (mon+1));

    //replace temporaray placeholdes
    str = str.replace("xxxx", this.weekdayNamesLong[wday]);
    str = str.replace("xxx",  this.weekdayNamesShort[wday]);
    str = str.replace("zzzz", this.monthNamesLong[mon]);
    str = str.replace("zzz",  this.monthNamesShort[mon]);
    str = str.replace("zz",   ampm);
    str = str.replace("z",    ampm.substr(0,1));
    return str;
},

formatNumber: function (num) {
  if (typeof(num) != undefined && num != null) {
    var parts = num.toString().split(".");
    return parts[0].replace(/\B(?=(\d{3})+(?=$))/g, this.strThou) +
    (parts[1] ? this.strDec + parts[1] : "");
  } else {
    return "n/a";
  }
},

//format number string $ # , . % 0 + R G - ( C
//mask can look like:  ($+R-G#,###.##%
//for minus, we will show minus unless user adds (
formatNumberObj: function(str, mask) {
  str += '';
  var splitnum   = mask.split('.');        //may have period
  var numdecs    = (splitnum.length < 2) ? 0 :
    (splitnum[1].split('#').length - 1);
  var hasDollar  = (mask.indexOf('$') >= 0);
  var hasPercent = (mask.indexOf('%') >= 0);
  var hasParen   = (mask.indexOf('(') >= 0);
  var hasComma   = (mask.indexOf(',') >= 0);
  hasComma       = (mask.indexOf('C') >= 0) ? true : hasComma;
  var hasPlus    = (mask.indexOf('+') >= 0);
  var hasRed     = (mask.indexOf('R') >= 0);
  var hasGreen   = (mask.indexOf('G') >= 0);
```

```
//FORMAT NUMBER FIRST - decimal points/comma
var num           = str.toString().replace(/,/g, '');
num               = +num;
if (isNaN(num)) return str;
var isNeg         = (num < 0);
var isPos         = (num > 0);
num               = Math.abs(num);
num               = num.toFixed(numdecs);
if (hasComma) num = this.formatNumber(num);
//ADD EXTRAS
var sfx   = (hasPercent) ? '%' : '';
sfx      += (hasParen && isNeg) ? ')' : '';
if (isNeg) {
  var pfx = (hasParen) ? '(' : '-';
} else {
  var pfx = (hasPlus) ? '+' : '';
}
pfx      += (hasDollar) ? '$' : '';
num       = pfx + num + sfx;
if ((hasRed && isNeg) || (hasGreen && isPos)) {
  num = '<span style="color:' + ((isNeg) ? 'red' : 'green') +
    ';">' + num + '</span>';
}
return num;
    }
};
```

Language localization

If your application will be released in other countries, or be used in this country by users wanting a language other than English, you will have to add a number of features to your program to support this feature. Steps include:

- You will have to determine which languages you will need to support. Then you will have to get all your phrases translated into each supported language. There are professional services that can do this for you.

- Create a file for each language that contains all of the language strings that you need in your interface.

- Remove all hard-coded strings that display in the interface and replace them with references to the appropriate string in your language file.

- Add a function to your settings page that allows the user to select their interface language.

- Add a function that gets called every time the app starts or the user changes the language on the settings page. This will call any registered handlers for any views that may have to dynamically change any strings that are currently displayed or are in the DOM.

Language example code

The following code is an example of one way to handle language localization in your application. There are existing libraries that you may also want to look at as well.

1. Set up some global objects

```
xLang               = {};
xLang.uilang        = {};
xLang.callbacks     = {};
xLang.curLanguage   = '';
xLanguage           = {};
```

2. Load your language specific objects

```
xLang.uilang['en'] = {
  vSETTINGS:        "Settings",
  vMENU:            ["Search", "Menu2"]};
xLang.uilang['fr'] = {
  vSETTINGS:        "Paramètres",
  ...etc.
```

3. Add the function to be called when user changes language

```
xLang.changeLanguage = function(newlang) {
  if (xLang.uilang[newlang]) {
    if (newlang != xLang.curLanguage) {
      xLang.curLanguage  = newlang;
      xLanguage          = xLang.uilang[newlang];
      //tell all views that the language has changed
      for (var name in xLang.callbacks) {
        xLang.callbacks[name}();
      }
    }
  }
};
```

4. Add a callback to each view that displays a UI with strings

```
xLang.callbacks["settings"] = function() {
  document.getElementById("eTITLE").innerHTML = xLanguage.vSETTINGS;
};
```

5. Initialize the default language for all views

```
xLang.changeLanguage('en');
```

11

Loading program files

There are a number of ways to load your program files—the HTML, CSS, and JavaScript files that make up your application. The method you decide on will most likely be influenced by the general use of your program and the variables that you want to optimize for. Some of the factors to consider include:

- You can use regular script tags in your HTML to load your JavaScript files. The general practice is to put these at the end of the HTML so that the UI will load and display as fast as possible. Most browsers will now allow multiple files to be fetched but they will block execution as they are loaded and parsed. There is an advantage to loading fewer, bigger files but these will block longer.

- You may want to delay loading some of your files that are not needed right away to provide a better user experience. You would include the `script` and `style` tags in your main HTML that will just load the bare code needed to display the first UI. The JavaScript loaded would contain the code to dynamically load the rest of the application as needed.

- You may want to programmatically load files so that you can load different files based on user settings or preferences. Your initial script file that loads can have conditional logic that uses config values or even the information in the URL to determine which files to load. This can be helpful if your application supports different branding looks.

- You may want to consider using a loader like `require.js` to load your files only when needed. This is helpful if your application may never need certain files loaded.

- You should consider combining your files together since there is overhead for each fetch. You can also compress each file using any one of a number of existing compressors or compactors. Using minified code can make debugging more difficult. I tend to use compressed code where the spaces and comments have been removed, but not minified code where the variable and function names have been changed. There is some potential danger with minified names in Javascript because of its loose typing and use of `eval`.

- You should also consider the effect of caching on your file load times. Caching common files that are frequently fetched may decrease your load times. The downside of caching is that new files that have changed may not be loaded. This is more critical when developing your app or if your code changes often.

Using a file loader

I tend not to want to use `require.js` because I normally want to load all the files I need in the order I want them when the program starts, or at least after I have been able to display the first screen. Using native JavaScript routines tends to keep the total code size small. I usually have a small `index.html` file that loads a small `index.js` file that contains the following file loader code. It loads all the files from an array of filenames.

The routine also has an option to ensure that cached files are not returned. If the variable `cacheBust` is set to `true`, a random string is added to the end of each requested URL to ensure that any cache is bypassed. The `filesToLoad` array contains the name and type of all the files you want to load. This array can be in this file or loaded from a config file.

If needed, you can also change the name or location of the files you are loading based on user settings or runtime parameters.

1. Set up a routine to add DOM elements

```
//IE
if (!window.addEventListener) {
  var createDOMElement = function(type, attributes, innerHTML) {
    attributes = attributes || {};
    var element = document.createElement(type);
    if (innerHTML) element.innerHTML = innerHTML;
    for (var key in attributes) {
      if (key == "class") {
        element.setAttribute("className", attributes[key]);
      } else if (key == "style") {
        element.style.cssText = attributes[key];
      } else {
        element.setAttribute(key, attributes[key]);
      }
    }
    return element;
  };

//ALL EXCEPT IE
} else {
  var createDOMElement = function(type, attributes, innerHTML) {
    attributes = attributes || {};
    var element = document.createElement(type);
    if (innerHTML) element.innerHTML = innerHTML;
    for (var key in attributes) {
      element.setAttribute(key, attributes[key]);
    }
    return element;
  };
}
```

2. Decide if you want to bypass cache

```
var cacheBust    = true;    //set to true to bypass cache
```

3. Identify the head element of your main HTML file

```
var xTag_Head     = document.getElementsByTagName("head")[0];
```

4. Set up array that contains details of files you want to load

```
var filesToLoad   = [];
filesToLoad.push({type:"js", url:"js/util.js"});
filesToLoad.push({type:"css", url:"css/main.css"});
filesToLoad.push({type:"html", url:"main.html"});
```

5. Set up function you will call to load all files from the array

```
var loadFiles = function() {
  var nextobj = filesToLoad.shift();

  //GET NEXT FILE IN LIST
  if (nextobj) {
    loadFile(nextobj,loadFiles);

  //ALL DONE
  } else {
    init();    //the function to start your program
  }
};
```

6. Set up function that acutally loads file

```
var loadFile = function(obj,callback) {
  var fileref;
  var newurl = obj.url;
  if (cacheBust) newurl += '?ts=' + (new Date()).getTime();

  //CSS
  if (obj.type == "css") {
    fileref=document.createElement("link");
    fileref.setAttribute("rel", "stylesheet");
    fileref.setAttribute("type", "text/css");
    fileref.setAttribute("href", newurl);

    //CSS FILES DON'T FIRE ONLOAD-SET TIMER TO CHECK IF LOADED
    var interval_id = setInterval( function() {
      try {
        if (fileref.sheet && fileref.sheet.cssRules.length ) {
          clearInterval(interval_id);
          setTimeout(function(){if (callback) callback();},10);
        }
      } catch(e){}
    },100);
    xTag_Head.appendChild(fileref);

  //JAVASCRIPT FILES
  } else if (obj.type == "js") {
    fileref = document.createElement('script');
    fileref.setAttribute("type","text/javascript");
    fileref.setAttribute("src", newurl);
```

```
      fileref.onload = function() {
        fileref.onload = fileref.onreadystatechange = null;
        if (xTag_Head && fileref.parentNode &&
          fileref.type=="text/javascript") xTag_Head.removeChild(fileref);
        setTimeout(function(){if (callback) callback();},10);
      };
      xTag_Head.appendChild(fileref);

    //HTML FILES
    } else if (obj.type == "html") {
      var req =  new window.XMLHttpRequest;
      req.onreadystatechange = function() {
        if (req.readyState == 4 && (req.status == 0 ||
          req.status == 200)) {
          try {
            var dv2 = createDOMElement("div",{id:obj.id,
              'class':obj.sclass},req.responseText);
            document.getElementById(obj.element).appendChild(dv2);
          }
          catch(e) {
            console.log("ERROR LOADING "+newurl);
          }
          setTimeout(function(){if (callback) callback();},10);
        }
      };
      req.open("GET", newurl, true);
      req.send("");
    }
  };
```

7. Now, start the loading process

```
loadFiles();
```

12

Tools

There are hundreds of libraries, plug-ins, add-ins, frameworks, and processors available to help you produce better apps in less time. New ones are added every month. You may want to use these to help shorten your development time, or to enhance your program. If you are working at a company, their policy may necessitate you using one or more of these packages. Most of them have active user communities that can provide documentation and help. This book is about writing native JavaScript without using any of these tools. Since most of these tools are essentially JavaScript themselves, learning native JavaScript should still be a high priority. Some of the issues that you should be aware of when using these tools include:

- Your choice of which frameworks and libraries you learn may influence your future job search since most job listings have strong preferences for these items. It seems there is always a new tool coming out that becomes the current favorite.

- There are often cross-dependencies between these tools where using tool A requires you to use tool B which may require you to use tool C. This adds more code and requirements for additional learning.

- They all have their own learning curve, some steeper than others.

- They all make your code bigger, though in many cases they just replace code that you would be writing from scratch. Other than some of the processors, they are all just more JavaScript code.

- Anyone else, now or in the future, that has to read your code will have to be familiar with the same set of libraries and frameworks

- You may need to keep using the latest version and keep track of which versions of each tool work with what other versions of the other tools you are using.

- You may often find that you have to make small changes to the third party software to make it do exactly what your application requires. You then have to keep track of those changes since you can no longer use new releases of the tool without changes.

- It takes a lot of research to select each tool you think you need. Once selected, you may spend a lot of time implementing it before you discover that it won't do everything that you need.

- You will need to decide if your application fetches all the third party code you are referencing from a remote server each time, or whether you will download the code once to your local server and then have the application load from there. There are pros and cons of doing it each way.

- The use of the tools discussed in this chapter can be helpful when working with a group of programmers who have to understand everyone's code, or on a project like a website that will have to be maintained for years. As long as everyone involved is proficient in the tools selected, they can help speed up development and reduce errors.

- Many of the libraries and tools may add a lot of code and slow down performance.

Frameworks

There are a number of JavaScript frameworks available today and new ones seem to be added all the time. They help define the structure of your program and help organize your code. Most of them are based on a MVC pattern consisting of Model, View, and Controller parts. *Angular* is one of the more popular framework and *React* is one of the newer ones. The frameworks are written in JavaScript and thus add more code to your application, but used properly they should help the amount of code you have to write yourself. They have their own learning curves and it is easy for inexperienced framework programmers to write really bad code. Most frameworks have an active user community providing many add-ins. Popular frameworks include:

- Angular
- React
- Backbone
- Ember
- Spine
- Ext JS

Libraries

JavaScript libraries are different from frameworks. Libraries make it easier to program many of the common functions in most applications. The most popular library is jQuery and there are many variations available for mobile devices as well. They make handling Ajax calls for communicating with the server simpler as well. They historically greatly simplified running the same code on different browsers as there were many differences that caused problems, particularly with earlier versions of Internet Explorer. These differences have largely gone away. Just like frameworks, libraries are all written in JavaScript and add significant amounts of code to your app.

- jQuery
- Zepto.js
- Prototype
- Dojo
- Knockout
- Underscore

You can see from the test below that some performance using these libaries can be abysmal. The following test compares doing a simple `document.getElementById` and `document.getElementsByClassName` with a simple jQuery equivalent. In some cases, the jQuery equivalent is 2,000 times slower. So I would be careful even if you have to use jQuery that you use native JavaScript calls where performance is a problem. The following test was done using `jquery-3.1.1.min.js` which was the latest jQuery library available.

⏱	PERFORMANCE TESTING	OPS (bigger is better)		
		Safari	Chrome	Firefox
1.	Native - getElementById	647	550	22,442
2.	jQuery - $('#id')	42	46	9
3.	Native - getElementsByClassName	660	401	20,049
4.	jQuery - $('.class')	9	3	3

Test 12-1: http://www.nativeJavascript.com/tests/Test-FixedArray.html

These tests also point out the tradeoff you make when you have any function that is multi-purpose. You can make the function handle lots of different cases but that is usually done with conditional logic that will degrade performance. For many uses, that tradeoff is worth it for ease of use and smaller code. For areas where performance is of importance, you may want to consider making specific use functions.

Templates

Templating systems help separate your HTML code from your JavaScript code and make it easier to populate lists of repeating elements. They use a special format that indicates where dynamic values will be used to populate the elements. Available template systems include:

- Mustache
- Handlebars
- jQuery Template
- Dust.js

Separating your display from your code is an oft-stated goal of many JavaScript enhancement products. On the one hand, you should not embed handlers and references to JavaScript functions in your HTML. On the other hand, your JavaScript should not directly create all your HTML. One way to consider this task is to think of the traditional skill sets required in making an app. The programmer should concentrate on the actual coding logic as they may not be proficient in the layout design. Whereas the designer concentrates on the layout since they may not be a programmer. The best tools would then allow for this separation. Too often, the template includes programming language, or the program includes HTML language.

CSS Preprocessors

These tools allow you to have more flexible and powerful CSS by accepting proprietary CSS input and processing it to produce standard CSS. The more powerful features include the use of variables and more nesting capabilities. Some popular tools include:

- Saas
- Less
- Stylus

The processors normally only compile the CSS up front and don't allow any dynamic changing of styles from the app itself if the user changes formatting options. And there are other solutions to substituting common colors or other values into your CSS or HTML. Plus, be careful that you don't overuse the nesting features as it can make your HTML very hard to debug and/or change, and it may run slower.

Polyfills and shims

Polyfills and shims are collections of code that allows your application to use features that may not be supported yet on all browsers. They let you implement these new features on browsers that support them, but provide a fallback method that works on the older browsers. They usually work by first testing for the existence of the feature before using it, and then using an older method if it does not exist. Some examples include:

- html5shiv
- PersistJS
- Modernizr
- Polyfiller

Minification tools

Smaller JavaScript code downloads faster, loads faster, and consumes less bandwidth. Since your code is not compiled like it is in most other languages, you need to take some extra steps to make it as small as possible. There are several tools out there that accomplish this using several methods including:

- removing spaces and comments
- shortening variable and function names
- replacing functions with inline code
- combining files into fewer, larger files

Your code is left alone and the compressor creates new, smaller files that you deploy on your website. Most of these steps are very safe. The more radical steps of changing variable and function names is also called obfuscation and has to be done carefully. Obfuscation will also make your code harder for others to use without permission. Most debug tools have 'pretty print' functions that can make your minified files easier to read, but they won't make any obfuscation clearer. There are also map files available to help you debug as well. Combining files makes downloading the code faster as there is some overhead involved downloading a file, no matter how small. Some good minifiers include:

* YUI Compressor
* Google Closure Compiler
* Microsoft Ajax Minifier
* JSMIN
* UglifyJS

> Be careful when using the more extreme minification settings as you might be introducing errors due to JavaScript's non-typed nature. See comments about this in Chapter 2 about JavaScript formatting. The more libraries you include in your code, the more important or necessary minification becomes. I have had code sizes quadruple when libraries were added with little gain in functionality.

Script loaders

Relying on `<script>` tags in your HTML is normally not the best way to load your JavaScript files. Each script will block your interface until it is loaded, and all your scripts will have to be loaded before your application starts. Using script loaders offers several benefits, including:

* loading some scripts can be delayed until your initial UI loads and displays resulting in a better user experience
* your code can decide which files to load based on config or user values allowing more customization

Some of the script loaders that are available include:

* yepnope.js
* HeadJS
* RequireJS
* LazyLoad

> Dynamic loading of script files can help improve the performance or perceived performance of your application. They are particularly helpful if your app often runs with only a subset of the total available files. However, their use may result in your scripts loading in a completely random order so you need to ensure that will not cause any problems. The user may also experience some delays as requested files are loaded.

"Any code of your own that you haven't looked at for six or more months might as well have been written by someone else."

-Eagleson's Law

13

Debugging

There are a number of tools available to help you debug your JavaScript/HTML applications. *Fire-bug* is a popular tool for debugging in Firefox, while Chrome has an excellent built-in debugger. Other browsers have built-in debugging tools with similar functions. I tend to use the Chrome debugger as I think it is the easiest to use, but you most likely will also have to run debugging tools on every browser that your application supports. These tools are helpful at every step of your development cycle but are particularly useful when debugging final performance and memory problems before deploying. Use them and use them often.

There are also other tools available like *JSLint* or *JSHint* to debug and format your code. Many errors can be found ahead of time by these tools and they help in making your code more readable as well. Many development environments, like Eclipse or IntelliJ IDEA, will perform these functions as well, many of them in real time as you enter code.

The available tools are well documented on the Internet and in publications, so I will not cover any tool in depth. However, I will touch upon the more important parts of the Chrome debugger that I frequently use when developing applications. You may want to research JSLint and JSHint for more information about how to use those tools.

Chrome developer tools

With your Chrome browser open, you can run the developer tools by clicking on its small `Menu` icon and selecting `More Tools/Developer Tools`. This changes slightly depending on your browser version and options. The tools should open up in a new window that you can position next to your browser window. The top of the window lists the various tools that are available.

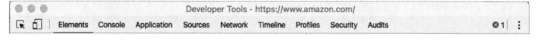

Toggle device toolbar

Clicking on the small icon in the left side of the top menu will display the current webpage in a mobile device emulator mode. This is very handy in seeing how responsive your application is when running on smaller devices. The device view will let you select exactly which device you want to emulate, such as an iPhone 6 or Galaxy S5. Click the icon again to return to regular browser mode.

Elements

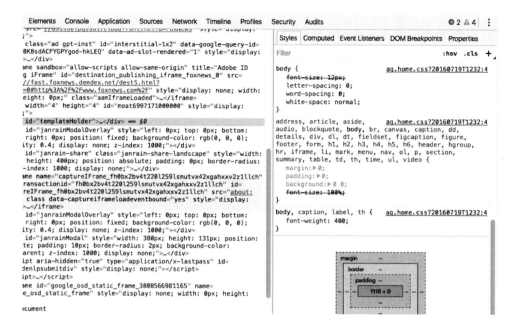

This is probably the most helpful tool on the toolbar. The `Elements` tab show you the entire DOM tree with all of the properties that have been assigned to each element due to your cascading style sheets and styles assigned directly to the elements. This can also be displayed by right clicking on an element in your browser window. and selecting 'Inspect'. This view is not the same as selecting `View Source` as that view is only the original HTML without any dynamically added or changed HTML. You can use the `Elements` tab to override any element or class property and immediately see the results. Simply select the element in the left pane and enter or change the property in the right panel. The diagram at the bottom of the right pane shows all the 'box' values of the selected element - the position, size, padding, border, and margin values. The top right hand pane is sub-divided into more tabs. The tabs used the most are:

- **Styles (default).** Lists all properties in the inheritance tree indicating from what CSS class and file they originated. Properties that have been overridden by a property in another class or style will be shown with a strikethru line.

- **Computed**. This will list the actual value of all properties after all inheritance rules have been applied.

- **Event Listeners.** This displays all listeners in effect for handlers like `click`, `scroll`, and `unload`.

Console

The `Console` tab is used for three main purposes:

- It displays messages from your application you have added using the `console.log` command. This can be very useful for displaying progress messages, version numbers, or values of variables when debugging.

- It displays system error messages including the filename, function name, and line number.

- You can enter commands at the bottom of the console to execute JavaScript code and see the values of existing objects and variables. To see the value of an object or variable, simply type its name in the console window. You can also copy objects and variables to the clipboard so you can paste them into documentation or canned data files. This can be very handy. Simply use the following command in the console where xx is the name of the object or variable. It may reply with '`undefined`' but the object will be copied to your clipboard.

    copy(xx)

- You can also paste in multiple lines of code like a function and execute it, or type in the lines manually ending each line with `Shift-Enter`.

Sources

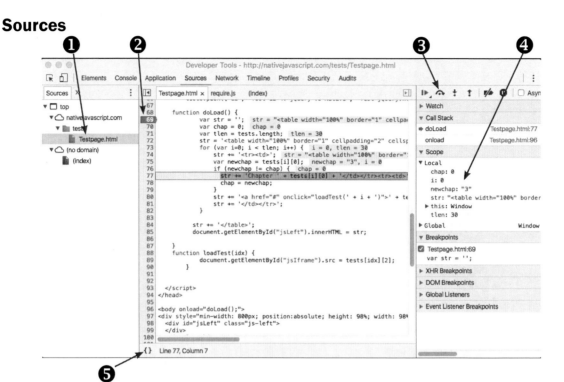

The `Sources` tab is your tool for line-by-line debugging of your code. After your app has loaded, you can pull up this tab and set breakpoints anywhere in your code. You can locate your JavaScript file in the upper left pane, scroll down to the line you are interested in, and then click on the line number to set a breakpoint. You can then run your code and the app will pause when it hits your breakpoint. You can then see the display of all variable values in the right hand pane as you use the control icons to walk through the code. You can also run the Pretty-Print tool (#5 above) to make minified scripts more readable. The available items indicted above include:

1. Select file to examine.

2. Click on line number to set a breakpoint indicated by the blue arrow.

3. Once breakpoint is reached, use these tools to walk through the code, including: run/pause, step over, step into, step out of, activate/deactivate breakpoints.

4. The values of all variables, local and global, can be accessed here.

5. Pretty Print minified code.

Network

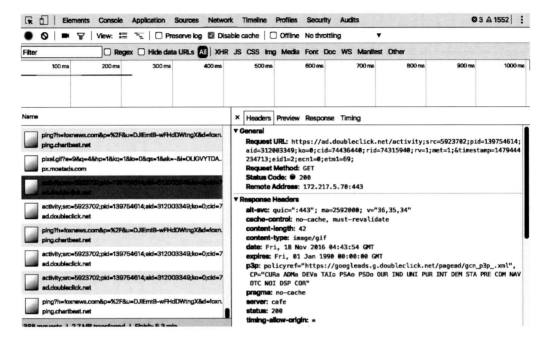

The `Network` tab lists all of the files that have been requested in the pane on the left side. You can see the full URL of each request and can examine all the details of each request and see the payload that was returned in response. This allows you to find mistakes in your requests or in the response. The list also shows how long each request takes to be filled. My most common usage of this tab is to right click on a file in the list at the left and select the 'Open link in new tab' option. That will issue the fetch again and show the results in a new browser window. You can only use this for `GET` requests and not `POST` requests. If you are loading JSON data, be sure to add a JSON formatter to your browser so that the object will be nicely formatted. Clicking on the Response menu item on the right will also display the results of the fetch.

Timeline

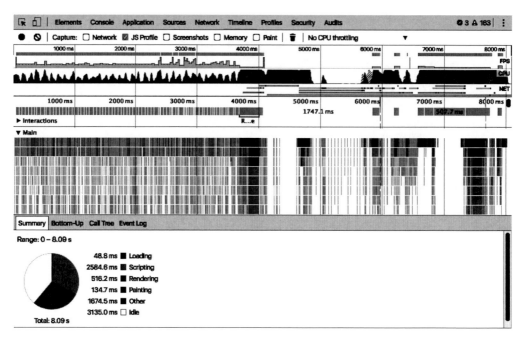

The `Timeline` tab gives you an easy way to profile your application looking for performance problems or even code that is executed by mistake. Simply click on the small circle icon in the upper left corner to start the 'recording'. You will see a small progress popup with a Stop button to press when you are done recording. You can then use the information on this tab to determine where your processing time goes.

Profiles

You can use the `Profiles` tab to track your memory usage and memory allocation over time. This can be invaluable in finding memory leaks or objects that take up excessive memory. The first screen displayed lets you select which type of profile you want, then you press the 'Take Snapshot' button to make a snapshot of the current usage or to start recording memory allocation. I find the 'Take Heap Snapshot' option the most useful in determining how large my memory allocations are.

Audits

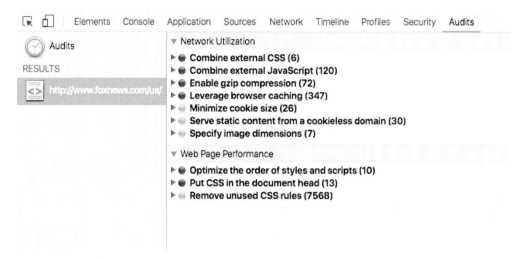

The Audits tab makes it easy to analyze your application for a number of performance metrics. It points out unused CSS rules, image tags without dimensions, and problems with your JavaScript code. Open this tab and press the 'Run' button to produce audit results for the current web page.

Loading files locally versus from a remote server

Be careful if you always run and test your software on a local server or directly from your computer. You may find that when loading and running the software from a server, the timing of file loading will be different and may cause errors. Asynchronous file loading results in an indeterminate order of loaded files so you need to be sure this will not cause problems, or take steps to control the order the files are actually loaded. You should also be careful if you only test your application on the fastest PC with the most memory. Most users will not have that configuration.

Debugging using console.log

Depending on your build environment and how fast you can change your code and reopen it in your browser, it is often useful to use `console.log` statements to help debug your code. Just place the statements where needed to indicate when functions execute, or the values of certain variables or objects. This may actually be faster than trying to debug the code using breakpoints. You may also need to use it to debug timing loops or code that actually executes differently if you stop it to examine values.

I often use a logging function similar to the following to display my console messages. It has some added advantages in that it can format the message, show only certain messages based on a config setting, and even display the elapsed time between messages.

```
//xLog.log(level, txt, brdrtype, timetype)
//level: corresponds to debugLevel
//0=don't display; 1-5: set according to severity or type of message
//txt: string to display
//brdrtype: 0=none, 1=asterisks above/below  2=hyphens above/below
//timetype: 0=none, 1=local time, 2=full date, 3=ms diff from last log
//Ex: xLog.log(2,"text",0,0);
xLog = {
  debugLevel: 2,
  logStrings: [
    "",
    "*********************************************",
    "————————————————————"],
  lastLogMs:  0,
  log:          function(level, txt, brdrtype, timetype) {
    if (level <= debugLevel) {
      var tdate            = new Date();
      var tms              = tdate.getTime();
      var diff             = tms - lastLogMs;
      lastLogMs            = tms;
      var pfx              = (timetype==1) ? tdate.toLocaleTimeString():
         (timetype==2) ? tdate : (timetype==3) ? "Diff: "+diff+"ms" : "";
      if (timetype) txt = "(" + pfx + ") " + txt;
      if (!console || !console.log) return;
      if (brdrtype) console.log(logStrings[brdrtype]);
      console.log(txt);
      if (brdrtype) console.log(logStrings[brdrtype]);
    }
  }
};
```

Common errors with closures

A very common error that is often difficult to find involves closures and the assignment of variables inside loops. You expect a variable to change based on the loop variable, but it actually displays just the last value. The following code snippet:

```
for (var i = 0; i < 3; i++) {
  setTimeout(function() {
    console.log("Regular closure: " + i);
  }, 0);
}
```

Products this output:

```
Regular closure: 3
Regular closure: 3
Regular closure: 3
```

There are several ways to fix this and similar problems involving variables being set inside closures. Here are 3 methods that you can use. The last one uses a fairly new JavaScript keyword call `let` used in place of `var`. You need to make sure you have the latest version of your browser to support this. All of these following snippets produce the following log:

```
Closure Fix: 0
Closure Fix: 1
Closure Fix: 2
```

Method 1

```javascript
for (var i = 0; i < 3; i++) {
  (function() {
    var j = i;
    setTimeout(function() {
      console.log("Closure Fix: "+j);
    });
  })();
}
```

Method 2

```javascript
for (var i = 0; i < 3; i++) {
  (function(i) {
    setTimeout(function() {
      console.log("Closure Fix: "+i);
    });
  })(i);
}
```

Method 3

```javascript
for (var i = 0; i < 3; i++) {
  let j = i;
  setTimeout(function() {
    console.log("Closure Fix: " + j);
  });
}
```

Proper error handling

There is a hierarchy you should keep in mind when designing your applications to minimize the impact of errors on your users. Remember that users generally will not put up with very many errors in your application before going elsewhere. The 80/20 rule usually applies to making your applications error free. Most organizations (and individuals) just don't have the time or budget to ensure their applications are 100% error free. Besides, this goal is usually completely unrealistic because of the huge numbers of variables out of your control. You can only test your app on a limited number of devices and operating systems. And each of the following items are out of your control and make error detection a n-squared problem with an essentially unlimited number of combinations of these items:

- Device: The exact model and OS version installed.

- Browser version: The exact browser type and version, including any options the user may have selected for their browser.

- Connection: Is this a 3G or 4G device? Or hardwired Ethernet or wireless Ethernet?

- Memory: How much free memory is available for your application?

- Other applications: How many and what other applications are currently loaded into memory? If you are designing something that works tightly with another application, then you have to test with every possible version of that software as well.

- Previous applications: What applications may have been run before and closed but may have left corrupted memory?

- Date: I have had applications that were fine until a certain date. A calendar program was tested all summer and worked fine but started have problems in mid-October. Before we could determine what was causing the errors, the errors stopped but started up again a month later. It turned out that a date field was not specified to be large enough and as soon as the date had a two-digit month and a two-digit day, it blew up. This happened starting 10/10/96 but stopped on 11/1/96. You just never know.

- Data. If you program allows the user to add or import their own data, then you have a huge possible source of errors. You need to test every data field for all possible combinations, including:
  - Empty fields
  - Long fields - as long as you can make
  - Unusual ASCII characters (!@#$%^&*(){})
  - Depending on what you allow, Unicode characters and extended ASCII characters like accented letters
  - Invalid field types, such as strings in number fields, or junk in date fields
  - Invalid entries in fields that have math operations performed - such as entering a huge number or a zero in a field that should have a number one or larger.
  - and so on....

- User interaction. It seems that half of the applications I have released after what I thought was extensive testing had problems with the very first user. This obviously meant my use cases were not complete. The errors usually surfaced because the user had some unusual (untested) collection of programs, hardware that had not been tested, or had simply entered unanticipated keys or run the program in an order that was not tested. This also drives home the importance of testing with real users as often as possible.

- Unusual key handling. Another hard-to-catch error condition sometimes surfaces when users press keys (or click with the mouse or touch with their fingers) in ways you have not tested. You really don't want to have a warning on each screen saying something like "Please press only one button at a time and do so very slowly and don't press another button until you see the results of the first press...and please don't hold down on the button." Users will do the unanticipated—click on the right arrow ten times very fast, wait 1 second and when they see nothing happen, click the left arrow ten times and then click the `Cancel` button. Can you handle that?

The point of the above items is that you can't possibly perfectly test your product for all possible error situations. So you will have to prioritize your efforts so you can get your product out the door sometime this century. You have to use your knowledge of the code and business requirements to determine which error conditions are most likely and most important. You should have a set of use cases that match this prioritized list. You will almost always ship your product with known bugs, but bugs you have examined and decided you can live with. The later in your development process you try to fix bugs, even minor bugs, the higher the risk of breaking something that you don't have time to detect. The efforts you should focus on, in approximate order, include:

1. **Prevent errors.** This involves unit testing your code as much as possible. Make sure each routine and module are as bullet-proof as possible, without adding excessive code to handle every possible contingency. For most functions, you will know what parameters will be passed in or what the possible error conditions might be, so be sure you handle those problems.

2. **Make it difficult for the user to create errors.** Add code where appropriate to prevent the user from doing something that may cause an error that may be hard to catch. For example, to prevent multiple key presses, you could have an alpha layer div (with an opacity of .5) that you cover the entire screen with after the user presses a button. This prevents the user from accessing anything else on the screen until the first process finishes. Likewise, you could disable the key, mouse, or touch-handling process until the previous event is completely handled.

3. **Make error conditions easy for the user to undo.** If you are unable to completely eliminate an error condition, then make sure the user has an obvious way to undo the operation or back out of the current error condition. This may be something like selecting a filter that results in an empty list. While not a true error condition, you should have a clear indication on the screen of what is happening and what the user can do next. Be sure to avoid always having obtrusive, modal popups that the user has to keep handling. That is a real drag!

4. **Add try/catch code where appropriate.** You can now add try/catch statements around your JavaScript code to handle error conditions. I would keep the following in mind when using these:

   ◆ Don't automatically put them in when you start coding as they may hide real errors that you should properly address.

   ◆ They do make the code run slower. They create closures around the statements which could slow down the code depending on what is in the closure.

   ◆ Don't rely on them at the expense of just writing the code properly to begin with. Use them for true, unexpected error conditions.

   ◆ They are most useful, and required in many cases, when you are handling external data that you have no control over. For example, if you are processing a JSON object that you fetched from a server, you may encounter error conditions that you can't plan for.

5. **Capture errors.** If possible, you can add code to capture error conditions (or for that matter, any user action) and log them or send them to a server where you can analyze the error and hopefully fix the condition in the next code release.

6. **Regression bugs**. These are the worst kind of bugs as they occur in code that you have previously tested, but code changes or other bug fixes create new bugs. Unless you have a complete plan to test for regression bugs, you are at risk. Even relatively harmless bug fixes introduced late in the development may have major consequences since you normally have less time to fully test the product again.

7. **Testing tools.** You may also want to consider using third party testing tools like Jenkins to automate your testing. These are particularly helpful in finding regression bugs when you run these tests after each code checkin. They mostly focus on unit-testing your code.

"Always code as if the guy who ends up maintaining your code will be a violent psychopath who knows where you live."

-John Woods

 Interviewing

The main impetus behind creating this book about programming was a wide layoff at the company where I had been working for more than 15 years. I was thrown into the job market for the first time in a long time. Plus, I was now a few years older and competing with Millennials that grew up with the Internet. I had been programming JavaScript and HTML for a long time but felt I needed to ensure I was acquainted with the latest methods and get reacquainted with the job interview process. So while I was trying to land my new job, I started on this book. Unfortunately (for the book) but fortunately for me, I found a new job in a few months. I am finally finishing the book and had some comments about the interviewing process that might help someone else looking for a job.

How to automatically be in the top 50% of candidates

I have been on both sides of the interviewing process—asking for a job and also interviewing candidates for work at my company. I also talked to the people who interviewed me as much as possible to see how I was doing and get advice for future interviews. I was continually surprised at how unprepared a large number of candidates were. So, independent of your technical knowledge required for the new position, I have a number of *Do's* and *Don'ts* that should get you into the top 50% or more of all candidates. At minimum, following these suggestions should keep you in the running. They may sound obvious to you but it is surprising how many candidates do not follow them. And these have nothing to do with your skills related to the new position.

- ❑ **Be on time!** Be late and you walk in the door with two strikes on you. Get there early to make sure you find the correct building and room...and it shows you are eager.
- ❑ **Resumé.** Bring extra copies of your resumé. Some interviewers may have lost their copy. You may also want to alter your resumé to make it job specific.
- ❑ **Dress**. Dress neatly but appropriately for the type and location of job. This may take a little research but it is better to be overdressed than underdressed as the saying goes. If nothing else, it shows respect for the interviewer.
- ❑ **Greeting.** Shake hands with a firm grip and look the other person in the eye.
- ❑ **Talking**. When you talk, be clear, upbeat, and positive. And speak slowly. Listen carefully to the question but don't be afraid to ask the interviewer to clarify any question. This shows you are paying attention and actually understand the area in question.

❑ **Answering.** Take your time answering questions. It makes you look like you are carefully considering your answer (and it gives you more time to come up with the best answer). There is nothing wrong with a pause in the conversation.

❑ **Writing.** If you have to write, write neatly.

❑ **Cell phone.** Turn your cell phone off. Don't even think about looking at it during an interview, much less answering it. No text messages either. Nothing will show lack of respect to your interviewer more than this.

❑ **Do your homework.** Find out everything you can about the company where you are interviewing. You can find lots of information online, at their website, and on financial websites. Make a folder for each job you are interviewing for and fill it with as much information as you can.

❑ **What job is this?** Know the requirements for the job for which you are interviewing. I am always flabbergasted that some candidates don't know what job they are applying for.

❑ **Give examples.** Be careful you don't try to take credit for something you did not do. But try to use specific examples of how you solved problems from your past.

❑ **Know your interviewers.** If possible, get to know the people who will be interviewing you. You can go to LinkedIn and get their bios and pictures if they have been posted. It will always be helpful to know their background and skill set. And you may find some common interest in hobbies, sports, or schools. Put that information in your folder also.

❑ **What happened?** Be prepared for some personal questions about why you left your last job, what did you like or not like about it, how you work with other people, what are your strong and weak points, etc. These are independent of the technical job skills but are just as important for most jobs as you will be working with other people. Rehearse your answers ahead of time. Your answers here may get you the job or keep you out of the running.

❑ **If you can't say something nice...** Don't ever badmouth a previous employer or any employee. Be prepared with a positive response to any questions about your previous jobs.

❑ **Benefits.** Try to avoid talking about salary or benefits, at least for the first interviews. These questions can come later if you are still in the running. You can kill your chances early on if you are asking about how many days you can work at home or how much vacation you get.

❑ **Ask questions!** You are interviewing them as well. You are making a decision about what you will be doing for years that will have a huge impact on your life. You need to find out as much as you can about the company itself and the people who work there. Ask direct questions about advancement opportunities and the corporate vision. You may decide that even though they want you, you do not want to work there. Plus, if you don't ask questions, most interviewers will treat that as a negative—they want you to inquire.

❑ **Follow up.** A polite e-mail to thank the interviewer will also keep your name in front of the interviewer and shows them that you are interested. I got feedback from some early interviews at jobs I was interested in that the interviewer didn't think I was interested. A follow up e-mail would have helped remove this impression.

- ❑ **Interview often.** Interview as many times as you can. You don't want to waste an interviewer's time if you know for sure you don't want the job but every interview will improve your performance in the next one. I know my first interviews were disasters until I got more experience. Plus it seemed that I learned something new from every interview or discovered an area I needed to study more.

- ❑ **Practice**. Practice answering interview questions ahead of time, including writing down solutions to programming problems. Answer questions out loud. You want to get used to speaking slowly and clearly.

Answering technical questions

Now we get down to how to respond to the technical side of the interview that probes your knowledge required for the job. I believe what is more important here than your answers is how you reason through the problem. In this age of having every answer available in .28 seconds using Google, remembering every option of every function is not as important as knowing how to identify the problem the software is attempting to solve and then designing a solution correctly. The most important things to keep in mind when handling this part of the interview include:

- ❑ **Clarify the question**. Make sure you clarify the question if it is unclear at all. Don't be afraid to ask questions so you understand the problem. Often your questions may prove that you understand the problem enough that you don't even have to answer it.

- ❑ **Verbalize your solution.** The way you approach a programming problem is often more important than the exact details. An interviewer normally won't penalize you if you can't remember the exact format of the `subString` method (or is it `subStr`?) but you explain what the function is doing.

- ❑ **Keep talking.** Don't just sit there speechless if you run into a problem. Talk your way through it. Often you may not even have to finish answering the question if your logic and reasoning is correct. It is easy to have *'stage fright'* particularly if you haven't interviewed in a while. Verbalizing the problem sometimes even helps you come up with the right answer, and it shows the interviewers your thought processes (and sometimes they may even help you.)

- ❑ **Don't make something up**. If you don't know the answer to something, don't make one up. If you can't remember the name of a method, just say so. You could even say something like: "I haven't had to do that but I can see how it would be important. Let me see...I think this might work..."

- ❑ **Be prepared**. Do your homework ahead of time. Make sure you study all the areas that you think will be covered in each interview. That is another reason it is important to know about each company and each job ahead of time as that will influence your areas of concentration.

General types of questions at interviews

There are a few general categories of questions that you might be asked. There are a number of books and blogs out there that list all kinds of interview questions, from very technical questions to weird trick questions. Take them with a grain of salt. A lot of them have good ideas but many go a little overboard. You will also find the same questions listed in a number of places as being 'common' questions. There is some value in looking at these sources as in many cases the interviewers are also looking there to find questions to ask candidates. But remember to learn the basics as many of the questions I have been asked have nothing to do with anything I have ever done programming. An interviewer told me once that if they had a candidate that could answer all of the difficult or trick questions, it probably meant that they had been looking for a job for too long and nobody wants them. The types of questions you will get include:

- **Experience/background.** What college did you attend; courses taken; degree achieved; etc. Make sure you don't exaggerate on this—it is too easy to check. A short summary of your work history will also be helpful.

- **Coding questions.** The questions will probe your knowledge about programming, in our case JavaScript, HTML, and CSS. The section below lists some common areas you should be familiar with.

- **Project management.** How well have you handled projects before, particularly those with multiple programmers.? Have you used development tools like Agile?

- **Behavioral/management.** Be prepared for questions about your working with former workers, how you solved work problems, how you handled difficult employees, etc.

- **Brainteaser/trick questions.** These are all over the map. Some ask you to estimate how many ping-pong balls fit in a car, others ask how many cans of paint it takes to paint the wing of a 747 airplane.. The ping-pong question normally requires you to make an educated guess, the airplane question might be answered simply by saying "One can - if it is big enough." Most of these have answers that are easier than you might initially think. Listen carefully to the question. These questions have value in determining how well you can problem solve or think outside the box.

- **Stupid questions.** "If you were an animal, what kind of animal would you be?" You're stuck with these if you are asked so just try to come up with a meaningful answer.

General questions

There are a number of general questions you might be asked that are not related to the technical requirements of the job. However, they are very important and your answers to these questions can be more important than any technical answers you give. Be sure to rehearse these ahead of time so you have coherent answers. These types of questions include:

- What are you proudest of in your career?
- What interests you in working at our company?
- What would you do if you won the lottery tomorrow?

- Describe times that you have worked well with your bosses and times that you have had problems.
- Describe yourself in a word or short phrase.
- What other jobs or companies have you been looking at?
- Why did you leave or why are you leaving your current job?
- What are some of your weaknesses and strengths?
- (*if appropriate*) You have been out of work for a while. What have you been doing?

Coding questions

One of the frustrating events when I was interviewing for jobs was that, no matter how hard I seemed to prepare, the interviewer always asked some question for which I hadn't prepared. This is another reason to participate in as many interviews as you can. The following list includes the general areas of expertise that you should know for a JavaScript UI programmer position. You will need to place emphasis on the areas that apply to the job for which you are applying.

JavaScript

- Object Oriented Programming: know different ways to create objects; how prototypes work; how to use the keyword *this*
- recursion: be able to program a recursive function
- Big O notation: know what this means and how it applies to programming. You should know this as many of your answers might need to take this into account.
- linked list: know how to make a linked list and when you should use it
- local vs. global context: the advantages and disadvantages; how hoisting works; namespacing
- event handling: bubbling and capture; delegating events; event propagation
- closures: what creates a closure and how you use them; how to properly reference variables inside closures; scopes in JavaScript
- sorting: how to sort in JavaScript
- browser detection vs. feature detection
- loops: know different kinds of loops and when to use each one
- module patterns: what are they and why you should care; how they can help keep variables out of the global context
- equality: know the difference between == and ===; using falsey comparisons
- DOM: accessing DOM elements using `document.getElementById`, `document.querySelectorAll` and and related selectors; what methods force a new layout of DOM
- strings: how to concatenate; what happens when concatenating strings with numbers
- objects, arrays, and associative arrays

HTML

- ◆ format: understand general format of an HTML page and its sections
- ◆ Semantic HTML: element names that reinforce meaning of sections
- ◆ DOM: understand how it is built and accessed
- ◆ Responsive webpages: know the concept of responsive sites and how to create
- ◆ Different ways to create HTML: templates; dynamic using Javascript
- ◆ Single page apps: what are these and why would you use them
- ◆ common elements: their tags and properties including `id`, `class`, `style` and `data`

CSS

- ◆ styles: using inline styles versus classes
- ◆ box model: what is it and why is it important; using `box-sizing` property
- ◆ centering: how to center elements in both directions
- ◆ pseudo elements and pseudo classes: how and when to use them
- ◆ properties: know common properties like `position`, `display`, `left`, `top`, `right`, `bottom`, `margin`, `padding`, etc.
- ◆ grouping and nesting CSS styles; descendant selectors
- ◆ CSS compilers: advantages and disadvantages of using Sass, LESS, and other preprocessors
- ◆ normalizing CSS: use of resets; `normalize.css`
- ◆ sprites: what are they and why would you use them

Server API's

If it is a vertical stack job, then you will need to know more about JSP/PHP and server side programming. The advice here is mainly for a UI developer that does not necessarily have to do server side coding. The popularity of `node.js` blurs the line between client and server coding and client-side coding. In any case, your UI code will most likely be calling the server to send and receive data so you need to be familiar with these items.

- ◆ JSON and JSONP: how are they different; when to use each one and how to process.
- ◆ `node.js`: how would you use
- ◆ synchronous vs asynchronous requests
- ◆ Ajax: fetching data; callbacks
- ◆ canned data: when and how to use
- ◆ caching: what is it and how can you control it; when to use and not use

Design Patterns

Know common design patterns for JavaScript and how they help encapsulate your code and make it more maintainable. Understand MVC patterns—model, view, controller.

Frameworks and libraries

The exact frameworks and libraries you should know and study will depend on the requirements of the job you are applying for. Knowledge of other frameworks and libraries will definitely help but make sure you cover any that are *required* for the new job.

- jQuery
- Angular, Backbone Bootstrap
- Templates: mustache, Underscore, HandlebarsJS

Buzzwords

There are a lot of names of programming terms, concepts, methods, and frameworks that you should know. Be sure to familiarize yourself with them but do not pretend knowledge that you do not have.

Other skills

- How to debug
- Know the general differences between browsers
- Project management tools. Have some knowledge about how to manage programming projects. Become educated in how Agile systems work.

Logic/Brainteaser questions

You may be asked one or more questions that are not directly related to programming but instead are intended to probe your problem solving ability. There are so many possible questions that you can't study them all, but most will fall into several general categories with similar types of solutions. Keep talking as you try to solve the problem, verbalizing your though processes. Remember that the interviewer knows this is not a question about a technical skill but rather a question that is probing how you solve problems.

- **General logic.** These require you to analyze the question and actually work through a solution. An example would be something like:

    ```
    You are given 8 balls of equal size. One of them is of a different
    weight—either lighter or heavier. Using a balance, how many weighings
    would it take you to find the ball of different weight?
    ```

- **Two answers - one simple and one complex.** These are questions that have two possible answers: one requiring a complicated mathematical or programming solution, and the other a fairly simple and obvious (after you know it) solution. Since you are interviewing for a programming job, it is easy to assume the solution is the complicated one. Just make sure you don't miss the easy one. This is actually a good test for a UI designer/programmer as simpler solutions are usually better. These questions might look like:

    ```
    Two trains are 100 miles apart and approaching each other at 50 miles
    an hour. A fly takes off from one train and flies 75 mph towards the
    other train and as soon as it reaches that train, reverses and flies
    back to the other train (assume no loss of time or speed to fric-
    tion). The fly keeps repeating this until the trains collide. How far
    ```

```
does the fly travel? The complicated answer would involve calculat-
ing each leg of the fly's trip and adding them up. The easy answer
involves just calculating that the trains would hit each other in 1
hour during which the fly would travel 75 miles which is the answer.
```

- **Listen carefully to each word of the question.** There are tricky questions that require you to carefully examine each word in the question to make sure you did not make any wrong assumptions about the question or any words in the question. The following question falls into this category.

  ```
  How many cans of paint does it take to paint a 747 wing? If you as-
  sumed that a 'can' means 1 gallon which is common in the U.S., then
  you will attempt to figure out how big the wing is and how many square
  feet each gallon will cover. Or, since the question did not ask how
  many gallons of paint, you could simply say '1 can - if it is big
  enough'.
  ```

FizzBuzz

I was hit with this at one at my first interviews. Since I had not done my homework and had not been interviewing for years, it was new to me. The problem is to write a routine that accepts a number and returns one of the following:

1. 'Fizz' if the number is divisible by 3
2. 'Buzz' if the number is divisible by 5
3. 'FizzBuzz' if the number is divisible by 15
4. Otherwise return the number

There are obviously a number of ways to solve the problem. I was surprised at the number of on-line comments about this exercise that stated that many applicants have trouble coding the answer. There are several important points to note here:

1. Any candidate for any programming position in any language should be able to give a fairly quick answer, even if it is not optimized.
2. The more important questions, at least for a JavaScript interview but likely for others, are your follow-up questions about optimization. There are a few ways the standard answer can be optimized for different goals, and probing the candidate's knowledge and solutions to those problems is very important. That would include questions about optimizing for speed versus creating garbage. One solution below does not create temporary strings in the calculation, but it is not necessarily the fastest routine.

   ```
   var fizzbizz = {
     str:    ['','Fizz','Buzz','FizzBuzz'],
     get:    function(num) {
       var a = (i%3) ? 0 : 1;
       a     = (i%5) ? a: (a + 2);
       return (a) ? str[a] : i;
     }
   }
   ```

Example questions

These are just a few random questions that I was either asked or that seem to be fairly common. You can find many more examples if you search the Internet but similar solutions apply to many of them. Many problems may have a brute force solution that may be workable but may be time-consuming or inefficient. You need to always pay attention and try to find a more efficient solution. And remember to keep talking as you look for a solution or write code on the blackboard. Some may involve considering Big O calculations.

Find minimum and maximum number in array

You are given an array of random numbers and asked to find the smallest and largest number. You could walk through the array checking each number but there are single line solutions shown below.

```
var arrNumbers = [1,4,7,3,5,9,3,2];
Math.max.apply(null, arrNumbers); // 9
Math.min.apply(null, arrNumbers); // 1
```

Reverse characters in a string

This problem gives you a string and asks you to reverse the order of characters. Again, you could write a loop that uses `substring` to build up a new string, or you could remember that strings can be represented as arrays with one character per element, and use something like the following:

```
var str = "abcdef";
var ans = ((str.split("")).reverse()).join("");
```

Finding descendants

Often, just rewording the question may point to a more efficient answer. I was given a problem of determining if element **B** was a descendant of element **A** in a multi-level tree. I first imagined a recursive routine that would get all the children of **A**, then get all their children, and so-on until I found element **B**. I then realized, with a little prodding, that I could just reverse this and quickly get the answer. Just start with **B** and walk up the chain to see if you end up at **A**. So the problem was reworded as "Is **A** an ancestor of **B**?"

Longest common prefix in an array of strings

This asks you to find the longest common set of starting letters in an array of strings, such as:

```
var arr = ["abcdef", "abc", "abcd"];
```

There are many ways to solve this by walking through the list comparing the starts of each string. However, an elegant and possibly more efficient (depending on the sort method) is simply to sort the array and then just compare the first and last element to see how many letters match.

Find the missing number

The problem involves an array of random numbers from 1 to 100 but only one number is missing. What is the best way to find the missing number? The best solution involves considering the Big O notation consequences of your solution. If you walk through the array creating a new array of flags, then you will need to walk through the new array again to determine which number is missing. This results in an O(2n) solution essentially meaning you may have to walk through all 100 records a second time (or until you find the missing number.) To make it more efficient, you could do the following:

1. Calculate what the total would be if all 100 numbers were present. This would be represented by `n(n+1)/2` or 5050.

2. Walk through the array once (O(n)) and add up all the numbers you find.

3. Subtract that total from 5050 to determine the missing number.

B
UI Design

Your job as a JavaScript programmer may not directly involve designing the user interface. You may have a different person or team that is designing the UI and you are simply implementing it. Or you may be in charge of both designing and programming the interface. In either case, you should be aware of the general guidelines, concepts, and best practices for computer interfaces. You don't necessarily have to be a graphic designer as well as you can easily get those skills provided by someone else. This chapter includes recommendations about UI design from start to end.

Single page apps

Traditional websites often are composed of separate pages that are linked together with hyperlinks. You load an entire page, then when the user clicks a menu button, you replace the current page with a new HTML page, reloading the required JavaScript and CSS files. This will result in some screen flashing as the first page is unloaded and the new one loaded and displayed. A single page web app works a little differently. You load all the HTML, JavaScript, and CSS files that you need and then hide and show the appropriate elements as the user navigates the site or application. You can still load content only when needed, but the important point is that you don't change the main global context so you don't have to reload code or reset variables.

Single page apps require you to spend a little more time up front designing your pages to reuse as much HTML and code as possible. If you have a common background used for all the pages or a common menu, then you don't have to reload anything and you will avoid any screen flashing. The same goes for loading the JavaScript code that will persist for the duration. Spend the time up front to design all the screens and functions of your application and your users will have a better experience.

General UI goals

There are some basic guidelines that you should keep in mind when designing any UI. They include:

- Clarity. Your interface should clearly display its information and have controls that are clearly separate from the data.
- Limit options. Having more than 5 or 6 choices on a screen makes it difficult for the user.
- Be consistent. All the screens in your application should have a similar look and feel, and all the controls should look and act the same way.

- Obvious usage. It should be clear which elements are controls and how they operate. Some new looks have move away from things like drop shadows, but they do convey information about the element. Likewise, if you have a control that looks like a slider, it should act like a slider.

- Obvious error or warning conditions with obvious solutions. Handle all error conditions. For the ones you anticipate, give a clear solution. And be sure to add ways to trap unanticipated errors.

- Give feedback for all user actions. Pressed buttons should change, selected screens should move, screens should dim when they are not active.

- Display progress indication whenever the application is loading, waiting, or thinking for more than a second or so.

- Provide online help wherever needed with access to more detailed help that can be loaded as needed or accessed on the Internet.

- Keep the interface as flat as possible so users don't get lost. Don't have nested levels of menus that require the user to navigate down and then back up.

Working with graphic designers

It is imperative to have your designers (those designing the screens, making your graphics, picking the colors) work very closely with the programmers. It is helpful if they also know enough about JavaScript/HTML/CSS and about your target devices to make the correct decisions as they design the screens. And, above all, they have to ensure their designs are optimized for a single page app. The worst case, in my experience (other than having no designer), is to have a separate designer or design team that designs Photoshop files in a vacuum, and then delivers a set of multi-layered PSD files to the hapless programmer. There is no reason that the designer can't provide you with proper CSS and final image files. Remember that not all Photoshop designs translate directly to CSS (like gradients) and, in any event, the programmer will have to spend time converting all of the other properties.

The designer must also stay very involved in the logic flow of the program. The entire app has to be thought through and all corner cases considered up front while you are designing the UI—don't wait until halfway through.

Corner cases

You will often see and hear of "corner cases" or "edge cases" when you are designing and debugging your interface. These are the problems that occur when abnormal situations occur or when users carry out some function or set of functions in a manner not normally used. Many times fixing these corner cases can be deferred if you determine that they will rarely happen or that the consequences are minimal. However, I have seen many UI designs fail because they ignored corner cases. These cases must be considered when you are designing your main screen interactions because they can easily invalidate your approach.

Start with use cases

The most important (and most overlooked) step in the development of a new application is clearly identifying what the application should do. This is best done by identifying the most common 'use cases' which describe the various tasks that your software should accomplish. The Agile environment calls them user stories. There are a number of systems in use that use various terms and methodology to describe these processes, using terms likes actors, goals, and systems. Your company may have specific requirements for how you should develop and document use cases—the most important thing is to take the time to analyze exactly what tasks your software needs to accomplish and how it will be used. Make sure your application:

- Accomplishes what the user needs to get done. You can add some cool features or special animations but just make sure that the important tasks are accomplished.

- Is usable by the target user. You need to take into account the skill set and experience of the user. Designing an application for the mass market has different requirements than one that would be used by chemical engineers, for example.

In general, you want to build up a number of use cases that cover all the expected usages of your application. Make sure you cover all of your common, expected actions and most of the anticipated corner cases. Each use case usually includes the following simplified items:

- **Name**: Name of the use case, such as: Make a Reservation.

- **Actor**: This is a user of your application who carries out a specific action. If you are designing a travel application, you may have actors for each of the following:

  - Person searching for best flight.
  - Person reserving flight.
  - Person accessing previous reservation.
  - Notifying person that flight is changed.

- **Actions**: Detailed steps to accomplish this use case.

- **Result**: A measurable result from the actions.

- **Priority**: Some indication of the importance of this case

You need to have the complete requirements for your application in order to make the correct use cases. Make sure your measurements of results are as objective as possible. Your result can't be "fast navigation" or "easy to use"—it should be concrete and measurable—"full page scroll in less than 2 seconds" or "95% of test users select proper menu item the first time."

Observe your users

Most of the times I have been unhappy with applications that I have released have been because I have not been able (or had the time) to sit with users and watch how they interact with the software. Sometimes a client has made it difficult to meet with their users; other times the schedule has been too tight to allow this. Even if you fit the requirements of your target user, you are way too close to the product to be a good test case. If you do have access, be sure to to the following:

- Learn how they accomplish the task today, either manually or with other software. Ask questions of each user: What are you doing now? What if this happens? What would make this task easier?

- Make a working prototype as early as you can and put it in front of users and then watch them interact and ask them questions. Do this as often as feasible throughout the process.

- You need to observe—don't rely on others to make the observations as they often don't know the right questions to ask and they don't know what may be possible with the software.

- Sit with users and watch them do their tasks or run your program.

Business rules or requirements

If you are developing your application for a client or company, there are usually a number of options or decisions called *business rules*. These affect how various parts of your app function and are usually put in a `config` file so they can be easily changed. You need to work with your customer to ensure you have included all necessary items. They usually affect areas where there are a number of different, but equally valid, ways to accomplish a task. The list often includes items like screen timeout times, password rules, logos, encryption of API's, etc. Be sure you get the customer to detail these as early in the development cycle as possible.

Models and metaphors

The user's conceptual model of how your application works must match the one you used to actually make the application, or you will have problems. Sometimes the problem is created by you, the designer, being too close to the application and making assumptions about how the app works that a user new to the UI would not make. You need to be consistent in your UI design so that the user will always know how buttons and scrolling work.

A very common UI design pattern is to mimic an existing metaphor that users may be familiar with. This can be a pattern in other popular programs, or even a real-life metaphor that has nothing to do with computers. The selection of a visual or functional metaphor for your program must be made very carefully. You should pick something that actually makes it easier for the user to access your interface and you have to be consistent with that metaphor. Examples of computer UI metaphors abound, including:

- **Index cards** (Apple's Hypercard, Flashcard programs)
- **Carousels**. Usually used for pictures that slide in and out horizontally.
- **Paper/Notebook pages.** Background images that look like paper.
- **Rolodex.** Most often used for list of addresses or similar items.
- **File folders/tabs.** Tabs are often used to page between screens of different functionality.
- **Books**. Often used to show spines of books on shelves to allow user to select and open.

Problems with metaphors

1. Forcing the logic of all your screens to fit your metaphor. If you have not thought through all of your screens, you may find when trying to program your last screen, that you just can't force the logic into your visual metaphor.

2. Picking a metaphor that may not be obvious or known to your users. It has to potentially work across cultures and languages. And does a magnifying glass mean search or zoom?

3. Consistency. If you have picked a metaphor to use in your application, you must be consistent. It needs to be used on all your screens and features. If you have a design where the screens rotate in from the left or right like a carousel, then don't suddenly switch and have some screens popping up from the bottom or fading in. If you are using a book metaphor, when you display pages can they scroll up and down, or is the user forced to view the content one page at a time? How do they get back to the table of contents?

4. Touch screen. An interface that runs on a desktop that uses a mouse, and a mobile device that uses a touch screen may have problems. If you have a long list that a user scrolls on a desktop by clicking on a down arrow, you can solve the problem of a long list by replacing the contents in the list. If the same list is display on a touch screen device, you need a better way to let a user quickly swipe the screen to display the entire list.

5. Other programs on same device. The popular programs that run on the device you are targeting may affect your design. Users on Mac computers are used to a different look and feel than Windows users. Users on an iPad, for example, are used to how the Settings screen looks and operates. Features in other apps may also raise the user's expectations of what your app should do. If you have pictures, the user may expect to be able to pinch them to zoom the display.

6. Be careful with metaphors that might just be too cute. Remember Microsoft's Bob application? It had a number of problems, one of them being it was just too cute.

Conventions are there for a reason

Use "conventions" to your advantage. If there are accepted ways that most users carry out certain functions, make sure you use them and definitely don't change them to something else. UI conventions let your users concentrate on your content, not the UI navigation. You want to reduce any mental effort a user has to exert just to navigate your site. Too much effort and your user will go elsewhere. Driving a car has become an almost mindless task (think eating that juicy burger while driving), mainly because the auto industry has standardized on how cars work, where the gas and brake pedals are, etc. These conventions work. If you need a way for users to buy multiple items and see the list of potential purchases at any time, consider using a "Shopping Cart" icon available at the top of each screen, as that is a widely-accepted convention. Don't call it "Buy List" and bury it on some menu.

I think some of the new Google and Microsoft designs are really a step backwards because they ignore these conventions in their attempt to make their UI's look "new". They remove drop shadows and gradients in controls so now it is very hard to tell what is a clickable control and what is just information.

A picture can be worth a 1000 words

Sometimes, having a small JPG or PNG image to convey a function is truly worth a 1000 words. You might want to use this in a settings type page where the user is selecting options that control the visual display—like zooming, page orientation, or whether an info panel is displayed to the right or below the main window. Just put a small image in the UI and the user will instantly know what you are trying to say. You don't have to worry about language localization as an added bonus. And you can also fit more action icons on the screen than you can text.

Chartjunk

Edward Tufte, in his wonderful book about design, *The Visual Display of Quantitative Information,* refers to unnecessary elements on the screen or in graphs as *chartjunk.* Don't add unnecessary elements on your screen. Embrace white space. It is OK to leave space around elements to aid screen readability in general. Make every element count. Instead of a separate sort button or buttons, allow the user to click on the column heading. Don't make graphs look 3-dimensional if that misrepresents the data. Remove vertical or horizontal lines that aren't needed.

Screens should self-document

The user should always be able to determine the state of a screen. They should self-document whenever possible. If the user clicked on a row in a table on one screen to see more detail, the detail screen should repeat the item's name from the first screen so it is clear what is being represented. This is more important in multi-user experiences such as software that will be run on a TV screen and viewed by more than one person. Don't rely on the person remembering exactly what they selected on one screen when you display the next. This can be done with extra text fields on the screen, small icons, or with special colors.

Function first—form later

Get your logic in place. Study the needs of your end user very carefully. Design the logic flow of your program first. Use a good wire-frame program to design and link all of your screens. Only then should you start laying on your visual design (eye candy.) I have often seen the process fail when done in reverse. Don't pick a metaphor first and then try to force the logic into that metaphor. I have found it more helpful to get all the features placed on the appropriate screens. Then, based on that layout and the expected user profile (is this for music or writers or gamers?) see if there is a metaphor that actually will help the user use the program. You don't have to have some cool-looking metaphor—you can make very effective designs that just leverage the standard interface appearance on the platform.

There is often pressure from management or sales to get something to show as quickly as possible which often leads to a graphic designer delivering Photoshop or Powerpoint slides without much thought to how the application actually needs to work. And those designs often have a life of their own. Make sure this doesn't happen to you.

Interface problems

- **Elevator bars on touch devices.** Elevator bar and scroll bars on traditional mouse controlled screens are very obvious. Everyone immediately understands how to use them and what information they convey. The `Down` arrow on the keyboard corresponds directly with the down arrow on the scroll bar or moving the elevator bar down. They all move down in the document. However, touch screens alter this obvious usability. To move down in a list, the user swipes up on the screen. If you display a scroll bar, it will move in the opposite direction. If you let the user grab the scroll button and move it, then that action will be opposite from doing the same thing over the text. You must be clear in how you display these controls and what you "invite" the user to do. And I really don't like "hidden" scroll bars that only appear when you start using them. Visible scroll bars convey a lot of knowledge to the user—that there is more data than is visible, what part of the document the current screen displays, how big the document is, and gives you a one-click method to scroll up or down by a page of data.

- **Spinners.** You may also have problems with spinners used for numbers or dates, and how the corresponding cursor keys are handled. If it is a list of dates, then does moving up go back in time (smaller number) or to a higher number (forward in time.) If you can, make date controls like this move from left to right. You will have a similar problem for channel numbers in a television guide. A `Channel Up` button may have the `Up/Plus` on the top of the button, but moving up in a displayed guide shows lower channel numbers.

- **On/off sliders.** These are popular on iOS devices but their use has spread. They can be very annoying if not implemented properly. Do I slide them to the side or just click on one side or the other? Do they even slide when moving the mouse?

Animation

The designer needs to be involved in this and it is very important that they can actually write the CSS that handles the animation. It does not help a programmer to give her a Adobe Flash file showing what the animations should look like—they really want the CSS that shows the exact transition, transform, or animation that produces the desired animation. Programmers often will not know the exact effect desired by the designers.

With the advent of CSS3, it became much easier to quickly produce all kinds of cool-looking special effects for screen transitions, moving elements around, or scrolling. However, there is danger lurking with these new effects, including:

1. They can be slow or jerky on devices that don't have the CPU power of your desktop computer. Having slow or jerky animations is most likely worse than not having them. Don't just test them on your high-end computer—try them on your targeted devices. Preferably, you will try out your desired animations in small test files before deciding to incorporate them. Remember, though, that they may still act differently once you have the code in the full app with a full DOM tree.

2. The animations should mean something. Don't have gratuitous animations just because you can. If the user presses a right arrow to display the next screen, then that screen should slide in from the right side of the screen. Likewise for other animations triggered by arrow controls. If you press a `Back` button, then sliding the previous screen in from the left will reinforce what is happening in the user's mind. If there is no obvious movement that makes sense, then you might want to try an opacity fade.

3. The more elements you animate at one time, the more you run the risk of jerky animations so try to keep them to a minimum. Keep your HTML simple. If you have a table of rows you are moving, try to minimize the number of elements in each row.

Envision your application used in a dark room

This applies to any UI designed for a TV that will be accessed by using a remote control, but the same concepts apply to UI's on any device. The basic rule is to design your interface so that if I have the remote controlling the television and you are sitting on the sofa but don't know what buttons I am pressing, you should be able to tell what is happening by looking at the screen. If you have designed screens to have no animation when the user presses the right or left arrow to look at the next/previous screens, then the other viewer will have no idea what just happened. Buttons should change shape, color, or position when pressed, and selected items should be clearly highlighted.

User feedback

There should be immediate reaction to user events. If a button is pressed or touched, the user should know immediately that the event was registered and something is happening. You can do this using one or more of the following techniques:

1. **Change appearance.** The button can change appearance as soon as it is touched. This may involve a color change, a size change, or slight movement. The traditional change on a PC or Mac program is to show the button as being depressed which usually means flipping the gradient colors. Just remember that on touch devices, the user's finger is most likely hiding any changes you make to the element. That is why many of the virtual keyboards show the character touched in a little bubble above your finger so you can see what key you pressed.

2. **Progress**. You can show a progress indication showing that something is happening. This is usually an animated `GIF` that is a small rotating circle or similar graphic.

3. **Show the next screen.** You should be able to show the next screen as soon as possible. Work on a design that lets you show the main screen elements right away and then fill in the rest of the fields.

You should also be sure to disable controls by dimming them or covering the screen with a alpha dimmed layer when you are processing the previous user action. Don't forget feedback when your application first loads. Be sure the user knows that something is happening.

Back button

If your apps are more than simply linked html screens, the use of the browser back button may cause problems. Many of the frameworks use # hashtags and URLs to move between functional areas. This allows the user to use the browser back button to go to the previous URL since it is in the browser history stack. However, that may not be what you want. In many apps, the screens are dynamically created and the correct handling the 'back' button is not clear. What happens in a browser if you save the screen as a favorite? What about running it later? Can you go backwards and forwards?

Screen size

You need to be aware of the screen size variations in your target market that you will need to support. These sizes can range from smaller sizes for small mobile devices to very high resolution computer displays. The items to consider include:

♦ **Minimum and maximum screen size.** If you are making an application for a company, they may have requirements for screen size support. If you are designing for the general public, you will have to determine what range supports your requirements. The minimum size is usually more critical as even 800 x 600 can be hard to support.

♦ **Mobile device size.** If you are supporting mobile devices, either by writing responsive web pages or an actual mobile application, then you will have to determine exactly which devices you feel you must support. You will most likely run on other mobile devices but this will be the list of devices you should be testing with your software.

♦ **Portrait vs landscape.** If you are supporting mobile devices, you may have to decide if you support them in both portrait and landscape modes. There are so many sizes for phones and tablets that the lines between portrait and landscape is blurred. However, there are a number of apps that will only run in either portrait or landscape on smaller phones. Your app may have wide lists that just won't work in portrait mode.

♦ **Responsive apps and web pages.** You should always write your applications to be responsive to screen sizes so that they automatically scale as the user resizes their window. You may make the app resizable to any size, or you may decide that there will be a minimum size (like 800 x 600) that you will not go below. Your app should smoothly scale up and down as the window size changes.

Double Negatives

Avoid double negatives as they can be confusing. Try to avoid options that say something like:

❏ `Hide comments`

or

❏ `Disable display of warning messages`

Colors

There are two main uses of color in your application:

- To reinforce a company or product line color scheme.
- To can convey knowledge to the user to assist them in making the correct decisions.

Your designer should come up with a limited palette of colors that will be used throughout your product. This is often based on existing websites or programs, and often incorporates the company's logo and trademark colors. Remember that most larger companies have very detailed and exacting specs for their corporate look. They will have exact color values for anything associated with their company name, and logos must meet their guidelines. Each color should be identified for exactly where in the interface they will be used, including:

- general display and highlight colors
- background color
- body text and body text emphasis
- url links
- headings and subheadings

Some areas to be careful of when considering what colors to use include:

- Be careful with your palette and selection, particularly if you get into very bold colors. There are cultural differences in acceptable colors, so you need to make sure you understand the target audience. Asian markets tend to be more receptive to very unique set of colors. If you are designing software that will be run on TV's, then the traditional approach has been to avoid saturated colors, even black. Do not use a solid red (#ff0000) and even your whites should be toned down—use #eeeeee instead of #ffffff.

- I really would avoid light text on dark backgrounds for large areas of text. It is fine for highlight and display areas. Another common color selection is to use dark gray for your body text. This can create a very distinctive look to your application or website. Just be careful your text is not too hard to read on the devices you are targeting.

- You also have to be careful if you have text anywhere that the user can select, as the selection may result in colors being inverted, for both text and background. Make sure that if there are any persistent selections that this inversion does not confuse the user.

- Colors can also have different meanings in different cultures. Be careful assuming that red means danger and green means OK.

Typefaces

Don't get carried away. This is one of the most obvious mistakes beginners make, whether it is in fonts for web pages, Word documents, or applications. There are so many really cool looking fonts available, and it is so easy to switch them, that you can easily produce ransom-note looking screens. Stick to a very small set of font families and use bolding, italicizing, and sizing sparingly and for effect. These fonts, sizes, and effects should be part of the style sheet that the designer creates for the programmers.

Feature Creep

Avoid feature creep at all costs. Keep your focus tight on the original business requirements for the product. Any additions should be justified only if they help meet those requirements. If you come up with new ideas, put them in your "Version 2" folder. A closely related area to avoid is design by committee. The more people that are involved with your design process, the longer it will take and the less focused your application might be. That doesn't mean you should avoid input from others—just be careful that you keep your focus and control how input is received from others.

Don't make obvious mistakes

I have seen too many screens on well-known programs that get the simplest things wrong.

- **Order of controls.** My favorite one is the use of left/right arrows (or prev/next). At least in western culture, things tend to move from left to right. Timelines move from older events on the left to newer events on the right. If you are displaying text as pages, then the previous page is to the left. If you have a horizontal list of anything (pictures, pages, etc.), put your navigation buttons in the correct order.

  Not: `Next|Prev` But : `Prev|Next`

- **Errors**. Make sure users can't get trapped in a loop, unable to carry out what they want, or even get out of the error condition. This problem could be something as obvious as the same error dialog popping up continually, or error conditions that don't tell the user what they need to do.

Learn from others

Don't beat your head against the wall when designing new functionality. Someone else has probably already done it, and they probably had a lot more money and people involved than you do. Learn from their designs—and their mistakes. There are lots of applications and websites that you can look at for free to see how they handled their UI design.

" First, solve the problem. Then, write the code. "

- John Johnson

Index

22223457R00102